Elite • 127

Japanese Paratroop Forces of World War II

G Rottman & A Takizawa • Illustrated by M Chappell & A Hook

Consultant editor Martin Windrow

First published in Great Britain in 2005 by Osprey Publishing,
Midland House, West Way, Botley, Oxford, OX2 0PH, UK
443 Park Avenue South, New York, NY 10016, USA
Email: info@ospreypublishing.com

ISBN-10: 1-84176-903-7
ISBN-13: 978-1-84176-903-5

Typeset in Helvetica Neue and ITC New Baskerville

Page layouts by Ken Vail Graphic Design, Cambridge, UK
Maps by John Richards
Index by Alison Worthington
Originated by The Electronic Page Company, Cwmbran
Printed in China through World Print Ltd.

06 07 08 09 10 11 10 9 8 7 6 5 4 3 2

A CIP catalog record for this book is available from the British Library

FOR A CATALOG OF ALL BOOKS PUBLISHED BY OSPREY MILITARY
AND AVIATION PLEASE CONTACT:

NORTH AMERICA
Osprey Direct, C/o Random House Distribution Center,
400 Hahn Road, Westminster, MD 21157, USA
E-mail: info@ospreydirect.com

ALL OTHER REGIONS
Osprey Direct UK, P.O. Box 140, Wellingborough,
Northants, NN8 2FA, UK
E-mail: info@ospreydirect.co.uk

Buy online at **www.ospreypublishing.com**

Author's Note

In this text Japanese personal names are given in Westernized
form, ie. individual name followed by family name.

Most linear measurements in this text are given in US/British
style; metric equivalent conversions are as follows:

feet to meters – multiply feet × 0.3058
yards to meters – multiply yards × 0.9114
miles to kilometers – multiply miles × 1.6093

Acknowledgements

The authors are indebted to Kenichi Tanaka, Tadao Nakata,
Takashi Doi, Harry Pugh of *Chute and Dagger*, William
Howard of the Technical Intelligence Museum, the
Yokohama World War II Japanese Military Radio Museum,
and the Kuteikan Airborne Museum, Funabashi.

Abbreviations

AA	antiaircraft
AP	armor piercing
AT	antitank
DZ	drop zone
HE	high explosive
HMG	heavy machine gun
HQ	headquarters
IGHQ	Imperial General Headquarters
IJA	Imperial Japanese Army
IJN	Imperial Japanese Navy
LMG	light machine gun
NEI	Netherlands East Indies
PT	patrol torpedo boat (US)
SMG	sub-machine gun
SNLF	Special Naval Landing Force
WP	white phosphorus (smoke shells)

The style (-) after a unit/formation title – e.g. 77th Inf Bde (-)
– indicates that some elements had been detached.

Glossary

General terms		IJA Raiding units	
Dai Nippon Teikoku Rikugun	Imperial Japanese Army (abbr. Kogun)	Teishin Shudan	raiding group
		Teishin Dan	raiding brigade
Kakku	glider	Teishin Rentai	raiding regiment
Kutei	airborne	Teishin Chutai	raiding company
Kuchu Teishin Butai	air raiding unit (abbr. Kutei Butai)	Teishin Hikodan	raiding flying brigade
		Teishin Hikosentai	raiding flying regiment
Kirikomi Tai	raiding unit or combat patrol	Teishin Hikochutai	raiding flying company
		Kakku Hikosentai	glider flying regiment
Rakkasan	parachute	Kakku Hikochutai	glider flying company
Rakkasan Hei	paratrooper	Teishin Koohei Tai	raiding engineer unit
Rakkasanhei Teppo	paratrooper gun (take-down rifle) (abbr. Tera)	Teishin Tsushin Tai	raiding signal unit
		Teishin Kikanho Tai	raiding machine cannon unit
Teishin	raiding (parachute) units	Teishin Sensha Tai	raiding tank unit
Teikoku Kaigun	Imperial Japanese Navy	Teishin Seibi Tai	raiding maintenance unit
Teikoku Kaigun Kokutai	IJN Air Service	Kyodo Teishin Rentai	training raiding regiment
Teikoku Rikugun Kokutai	IJA Air Service	Kakku Hohei Rentai	glider infantry regiment
Tokubetsu Rikusentai	Special Naval Landing Force	Kakku Hohei Chutai	glider infantry company
Yugekitai	guerrilla unit	Hikojo Chutai	airfield company

JAPANESE PARATROOP FORCES IN WORLD WAR II

INTRODUCTION

Although some countries conducted small scale demonstration jumps in the late 1920s, it was another decade before fledgling airborne units – deliverable by parachute, glider or transport aircraft – were raised by most of the principal belligerents on the eve of World War II. Only Germany and the USSR possessed significant tactical units in 1939. Japan – like the USA, Britain and Italy – began organizing such forces only after early German successes in spring 1940.

The Imperial Japanese Army and Navy were rivals in this, as in other fields. This tendency to develop unnecessarily similar capabilities applied to their airborne forces, which pursued no coordination other than the dual use of some equipment items. Each conducted successful parachute operations on a modest scale in 1942; others were planned, but were cancelled because of rapidly changing situations. Since Japan was forced on to the defensive from late 1942, no further airborne operations were conducted until late 1944 and early 1945, and even those consisted mainly of air-landed raids on airfields.

Apart from the operations actually carried out, however, the potential threat posed by Japanese airborne forces did have the effect of tying down Allied assets. For example, on December 8, 1941, the Philippine Division was ordered to move from Ft McKinley on Luzon and prepare defenses at Bamban–Arayat; a report of paratroopers landing – which proved false – led to the division being diverted to Clark Field.

Little has been written in the West on Japanese airborne forces. Most of what is known and accepted is based on wartime intelligence reports, mainly from a US Military Intelligence Division study, *Japanese Parachute Troops, Special Series No.32*, published in July 1945. While much of the information in this booklet is correct, there are errors and misassessments throughout, and some of these have been repeated elsewhere. For example, that study states that "About 100 German

An IJN paratrooper of Lt(jg) Yamabe's 1001st Experimental Research Unit at Yokosuka in early 1941, when they were still experimenting with equipment and jump techniques. This jumper wears a ripcord-opened Type 97 (1937) seat-type pack. Note the cramped exit position forced on the jumper by the small door of the Type 96 "Tina" transport, which slowed the jumping of sticks of paratroopers and thus increased their dispersal on the drop zone.

instructors had arrived in the fall of 1941." In fact Germany provided no assistance with parachute instruction or doctrinal development; the Japanese developed their own training and operational techniques, equipment, organization and doctrine, although much was certainly based on studies of published accounts and attaché reports of foreign experience. The US MID study mentions large numbers of parachute centers in Japan, Manchuria and China, training almost 15,000 paratroopers between January 1941 and the end of that year. These figures are greatly exaggerated, and probably based on intentionally misleading articles in Japanese publications. The same study also describes Japanese parachute operations in Hunan Province, China, in 1943 and 1944; in fact, no such operations were ever mounted in China, although parachute cargo drops certainly took place on quite an impressive scale.

Origins of IJA parachute units

It is stated that Gen Hideki Tojo, War Minister and Chief of the Army General Staff, was responsible for the raising of IJA paratroopers. Much impressed by the successes of German Fallschirmjäger, he directed the IJA to organize similar forces, and the first Raiding Training Unit was raised in December 1940 at the IJA flight school at Hamamatsu airbase on the south coast of Honshu. Ten IJA Air Service officers gathered as the cadre under LtCol Keigo Kawashima. None of the officers of this secret "Kawashima Unit" had any parachuting experience, but they studied all available information, and proposed training and tactical techniques. They dropped dummies in parachute trials, and wrote a basic manual before undertaking live jumps for the first time on February 20, 1941.

In mid February, 250 trainees joined the unit at Ichigaya airbase, Tokyo, where half of the unit had moved. All these volunteers were

non-commissioned officers, in order to form a leadership and instruction cadre; with the second class, privates also entered the unit. Initial physical fitness training was based on the belief that paratroopers required the agility of gymnasts to avoid landing injuries, resulting in the unit's early nickname of the "Kawashima Circus." Most volunteers were 20–25 years of age; the maximum age for officers was 28, though regimental officers could be up to 35. Most officers were assigned to the IJA Air Service; for example, Col Kawashima would go on to command the 1st Raiding Flying Brigade (see below).

After intense physical preparation the trainees undertook ground instruction for parachuting. In March 1941 the training site was moved to Tokorozawa near Tokyo, where equipment for jumping and landing training was set up. There were few ways to simulate a parachute descent, but one was found at Tokyo's Tamagawa amusement park. This possessed a 165ft parachute jump tower: thrill-seekers were attached to a canopy that was hoisted by cable before being released to float to the ground. Because the existence of the paratroop unit was secret, trainees were directed to visit the park disguised as university students, to experience a couple of simulated descents.

Each trainee at Hamamatsu subsequently made four jumps. For the first, they dropped individually; in the second they dropped one after another at intervals; the third was a group drop, and the fourth jump was made with arms and equipment. At first they used the same

Hauled up to the rafters of a hangar, a trainee demonstrates the exit position. The class wear long-sleeved jump smocks over white fatigue uniforms, and IJN Type 1 Special parachute harness. Note the forward-tilted position forced on the jumper by the single-point suspension behind the shoulders, and the inability to exercise control by gripping the lines – weaknesses shared by the contemporary German rig.

Like most other transports, the Mitsubishi Type 96 "Tina" used extensively by the IJN was a conversion of a bomber design, the G3M "Nell".

parachutes as provided to aircrews. These proved unsatisfactory, leading to the development of the Type 1 (1941) parachute specifically for paratroopers, and this was ready in time for use by the third and subsequent classes at Hamamatsu (see 'Parachutes' below.) The Nakajima Type 97 "Thora" transport was used for training jumps; derived from the Douglas DC-2, this accommodated only seven jumpers, thus limiting its usefulness to training rather than operations.

In May 1941, Gen Tojo transferred the unit to Baichengzu, Manchuria, as the Hamamatsu school became too small for the growing numbers of paratroops. The rationale was that Manchuria's remoteness would help preserve the secrecy surrounding this new force; however, it was inconvenient for the constant communication with other departments that was necessary during the development of equipment, and in August they returned to Japan to be stationed at Nyutabaru in Miyazaki Prefecture on Kyushu. Nyutabaru would remain the IJA parachuting center throughout the war.

With five classes trained, the 1st Raiding Regiment (*Dai 1 Teishin Rentai*) was organized on December 1, 1941, from 800 graduates of the first, second and third classes. Days later the 1st Raiding Brigade HQ and 1st Raiding Transport Unit were also formed, the brigade being commanded by Col Seiichi Kume. The 2nd Raiding Regt was organized in January 1942 from the fourth and fifth classes.

Origins of IJN parachute units

In November 1940 a small study and trials unit was established at Yokosuka naval air station on Tokyo Bay. The project designation was *1001 Go Jikken Kenkyu* (1001st Experimental Research Unit), and it consisted of 26 men under Lt(jg) Masao Yamabe. They began parachuting trials using dummies, and the first live jump took place on January 15, 1941. Like their IJA counterparts, they initially used unsuitable aircrew emergency parachutes.

The IJN maintained a large shore organization to operate and defend overseas naval installations; collectively, these base forces and

IJN trainees jump from a Type 96 transport with ripcord-opened parachutes. Besides the real concern of a jumper failing to pull the cord, the main problem with employing an aircrew escape pack for paratroopers was that the jumper had to achieve and maintain a stable position as it deployed – which was difficult when jumping from relatively low altitude and laden with equipment. A paratrooper who is tumbling as his rig deploys runs a real risk of becoming entangled in the suspension lines or wrapped in the canopy, with potentially fatal results.

guard forces were known as Land Forces *(Rikujo Butai)*. Among the Land Forces were Special Naval Landing Forces *(Tokubetsu Rikusentai)*, which were battalion-size units intended for seizing naval bases and spearheading amphibious assaults (it is incorrect to refer to the SNLF as "Imperial Marines".) The two IJN parachute units subsequently formed were part of the SNLF; in the usual way the unit designations were prefixed with the name of the naval base at which they were raised – in this case, Yokosuka.

In June 1941 the unit moved to the IJN's Tateyama ordnance school on Tokyo Bay, and started training volunteers, who were required to be under 30 years of age with at least two years' service. In September the Navy Minister ordered the formation of two parachute units of 750 men each, to be activated as early as November 1941. To train 1,500 paratroopers in such a short time was very challenging; the first and second classes lasted just one week and ten days, respectively, and subsequent intakes were rushed through two-week courses. A day's instruction consisted of two hours' gymnastics, one hour of trapeze and jump practice, three hours of parachute maintenance, and a one-hour lecture on some aspect of parachuting.

After this preparation trainees advanced to actual jumps. First, they dropped a dummy with a parachute that they had packed themselves, as a confidence-building step; then they made a total of six jumps. Close to the sea, Tateyama was subject to strong winds; several men died when they were caught in squalls or landed in the water. After completing their difficult and dangerous training, two parachute units were formed on November 15 at Yokosuka naval district base: the Yokosuka 1st SNLF (Cdr Toyoaki Horiuchi), and Yokosuka 3rd SNLF (LtCdr Koichi Fukumi) – sometimes referred to as the Horiuchi and Fukumi Forces respectively.

ORGANIZATION

IJA Raiding units

While paratroopers were called *Rakkasan Hei*, the collective IJA term for airborne forces was *Teishin*, literally meaning "dash forward" or "dangerous advance" – cavalry raiders had used the term in this context during the 1904–05 Russo-Japanese War. *Teishin* is generally translated as "raiding", and in World War II the term *Kuchu Teishin Butai* (Air Raiding Units) collectively designated IJA parachute, glider, and dedicated flying transport units; it was abbreviated as *Kutei Butai*.

Unlike the IJA's standard 3,800-man infantry regiment of three 1,100-man battalions, the raiding regiment was a battalion-size unit of some 700 men commanded by a major or lieutenant-colonel; it was organized as a light infantry battalion, with rifle companies about 160 strong and rifle platoons of about 34 men. Once fully organized in early 1942, the 1st Raiding Brigade *(Dai 1 Teishin Dan)* consisted of two parachute regiments, and an organic air transport regiment:

1st Raiding Brigade
Brigade HQ (Col Seiichi Kume)
    1st Raiding Regt (Maj Takeo Takeda)
    2nd Raiding Regt (Maj Takeo Komura)
Raiding Flying Regt (Maj Akihito Niihara)
    4 transport companies (each 12× Tachikawa Type 1 "Hickory" or Mitsubishi Type 100 "Topsy" a/c)
    Airfield Company

Raiding Regiment, 1942
Regimental HQ
1st, 2nd & 3rd rifle companies, each:
    Company HQ
    3 rifle platoons, each 3 rifle sections;
        1x LMG, 2× or 3× grenade dischargers
    HMG platoon (2× HMGs, or more when deployed)

The Mitsubishi Ki-57 Type 100 "Topsy" was widely used as a paratroop transport by the IJA, and to some extent by the IJN also, as the Type 0 transport. This is an aircraft of the airline Dai Nippon Koku KK, which also took military transport contracts. (Mainichi Newspapers)

Antitank gun section (1× 3.7cm AT gun, *or* 1× 2cm AT rifle,
    or 1× 3.7cm infantry gun)
4th Engineer Company:
  Company HQ
  3 engineer platoons (flamethrowers, demolition charges)

The unique difference from the airborne forces of other armies – the possession of organic transport units – helped expedite both training and operational jumps, ensured effective training of aircrews, improved mission coordination, and increased the solidarity between units. However, during actual operations non-organic flying units often had to be relied upon, as the organic units had not deployed. Mr Sato, who was engaged with the organization of the early IJA parachute units, shed additional light on this subject: "Even after the Pacific War began, some IJA transports were hired from civil airlines. So it was difficult to justify forming flying units solely as troop transport units. However, it was easily allowed if the unit was to be assigned to a raiding force." This statement needs some explanation. The IJA traditionally made limited use of transport aircraft. All resources were mainly dedicated to offensive units, both ground and air. IJA generals, preoccupied by the doctrine of attack, found the "raiding" designation appealing, and responded favorably to requests for allocation of transport resources to a "raiding" flying regiment.

Men of the IJA 1st Raiding Brigade board a "Topsy" transport for a training jump, wearing the pale olive long-sleeved jump smock apparently over the light tan one-piece jump suit. The orange Type 1 parachute packs with dark green trim and harness stand out in sharp contrast. Note also the red tail insignia of the 1st Raiding Brigade, later retained by the 1st Raiding Group (see Plate A). The aircraft is camouflaged with green dappling over its aluminum surfaces.

IJA paratroopers boarding a camouflage-painted Kawasaki Ki-56 Army Freight Transport Type 1 "Thalia", which was employed as a secondary type of Army transport; this aircraft was a copy of the Lockheed Model 18 Lodestar.

From brigade to quasi-division

The 1st Raiding Bde remained the principal IJA parachute force until November 21, 1944, when the 1st Raiding Group *(Dai 1 Teishin Shudan)* was organized by consolidating existing units. The Group designation was chosen because the assets were not available for a full division. It was a division-equivalent command, however, since it had a strength of approximately 12,000 men.

The commander of the 1st Raiding Group was MajGen Rikichi Tsukada, who had served in infantry assignments until the IJA Air Service began expanding and he undertook flight training. He had experience as a flight instructor, on staffs at various levels from brigade to army during the 1930s, and in command of an air regiment and an air brigade. Serving as chief-of-staff of the 3rd Air Army from February 1944, he took command of the Raiding Training Unit that August; his broad experience made him a logical choice to command a combined infantry and flying formation with a strategic reach.

While the 1st Raiding Group had a structure paralleling that of a division *(shidan)*, its capabilities were far inferior. Its six raiding and glider infantry "regiments" were basically only light infantry battalions, smaller than the nine infantry battalions assigned to standard divisions. It lacked any form of artillery, possessed only minimal combat support units, and relied on external logistical and service support. The group's equivalent of "divisional units" were organized as small two-company battalions or as single companies; they were not parachute trained, depending upon delivery by glider or transport aircraft.

1st Raiding Group, 1944
Group HQ (MajGen Rikichi Tsukada)
1st Raiding Bde (Col Isamu Nakamura)
  1st Raiding Regt (LtCol Hideo Yamada)
  2nd Raiding Regt (LtCol Kunio Oosaki)

2nd Raiding Bde (Col Kenji Tokunaga)
    3rd Raiding Regt (Maj Tsuneharu Shirai)
    4th Raiding Regt (Maj Chisaku Saida)
1st Glider Inf Regt (Maj Haruichi Yamamoto)
2nd Glider Inf Regt (Maj Saburo Takaya)

1st Raiding Flying Bde (Col Keigo Kawashima)
    1st Raiding Flying Regt (LtCol Akihito Niihara)
    2nd Raiding Flying Regt (Maj Kan Toda)
    1st Glider Flying Regt (LtCol Sonfuku Kitaura)
    1st Raiding Flying Bde Signal Unit
    101st–103rd Airfield Companies

1st Raiding Engineer Unit (Maj Ryuichi Fukumoto)
1st Raiding Signal Unit (Capt Hisayoshi Sakagami)
1st Raiding Machine Cannon Unit (Capt Kazuo Tamura)
1st Raiding Maintenance Unit (Maj Kenji Isami)
1st Raiding Tank Unit (Maj Kenichi Tanaka)

Raiding Regiment, 1944
Regimental HQ
1st, 2nd & 3rd rifle companies
Engineer company
Heavy weapons company:
    Company HQ
    AT gun platoon (4× 3.7cm AT guns/8cm mortars)
    Infantry gun platoon (4× 7cm infantry guns)
    MG platoon (2× HMGs)

Army *Rakkasan Hei* cramped inside a small transport type, a Tachikawa Type LO "Thelma", based on the Lockheed Model 14 Super Electra. They may be testing the feasibility of jumping with rifles, which are carried here wrapped in cloth. Note the cloth-covered steel helmets, and the smock's collar fastening tab. The helmet was secured by strong tie-tapes anchored to the clothliner, under the side pieces which fastened with a leather strap passing back and forth through two steel rings on the left side. Small cloth pads were attached to the liner inside the edge of the steel skull.

Japan developed several models of gliders, mostly for training use; the standard transport type was this Kokusai Ku-8 Type 4 "Gander". No glider assaults were actually carried out by the Raiding Group's 1st Glider Flying Regt, but elements were used to fly critical cargoes – radios, weapons, aircraft parts, etc – from Japan to Manila in the Philippines between May and October 1944.

The raiding regiment had 816 men, armed with 455× 7.7mm Type 2 rifles, 769× 8mm Type 94 pistols, 27× 7.7mm Type 99 LMGs, 6× 7.7mm Type 92 HMGs, 4× 7cm Type 92 infantry guns, 4× 3.7cm Type 94 AT guns *or* 4× 8cm Type 97 trench mortars in lieu. The engineer company was no longer designated the "4th"; and a weapons company was added to concentrate crew–served weapons. The engineer company had Type 3 (1943) flamethrowers and explosives.

The glider infantry regiments were organized from the 5th Raiding Regt, which had been raised in August 1943. The glider infantrymen were reassigned from standard infantry units and did not receive parachute training.

Glider Infantry Regiment, 1944
Regimental HQ
1st, 2nd & 3rd rifle companies
Engineer company
AT gun company (4× 4.7cm AT guns)
Mountain gun company (4× 7.5cm mtn guns)

The 1st Raiding Engineer Unit was also glider-borne. It consisted of a small headquarters, two engineer companies and an equipment platoon, with light engineer equipment and Type 95 light trucks. The similar 1st Raiding Signal Unit had a headquarters, a wire company and a radio company; telephone and radio teams would be attached to the group's regiments and other elements. The 1st Raiding Machine Cannon Unit was a company equipped with six 2cm Type 98 automatic cannons for employment against air and ground targets. The 1st Raiding Maintenance Unit had a headquarters, an air maintenance company and a ground maintenance company.

The IJA had studied the concept of airlifting a light tank by glider, and had developed the large Kokusai Ku-7 glider of 7 tons capacity, but only two of these were actually built. The 1st Raiding Tank Unit was intended to provide the group with a degree of mobile firepower; it had a single tank company and an infantry company, making it a small combined maneuver unit. The motorcar company provided mobility to the infantry company and elements of the glider regiments, and was under the tank unit's control mainly for convenience of vehicle maintenance. The antitank company was formed in 1945 with 12× Type 94 tankettes to tow the four 4.7cm Type 1 guns, and to haul ammunition in Type 94 full-tracked trailers of ¾ ton capacity.

1st Raiding Tank Unit, 1944
Unit HQ (2× Type 2 light tanks)
Tank company (12× Type 2 light tanks)
Infantry company
AT gun company (4× 4.7cm AT guns, 12× Type 94 tankettes)
Motorcar company (approx. 60× Type 95 light trucks)
Depot unit (maintenance)

The two raiding flying regiments each consisted of three transport companies, each with nine-plus Type 100 "Topsy" transports and one Nikajima Type 100 "Helen" heavy bomber for cargo drops. The 1st Glider Flying Regt had three companies each equipped with nine Type 100 bombers to tow its 18× Ku-8 Type 4 "Gander" gliders.

Naval parachute units

The Yokosuka 1st and 3rd Special Naval Landing Forces were 750-man units organized along the lines of light infantry battalions (other SNLFs were usually larger and more heavily armed.) The strength of the component sub-units is unknown. The HQ company had approximately 150 all ranks in its six platoon- and section-sized "units", and the command platoon consisted of reconnaissance, signal and messenger sections. Each rifle company had some 140 men; the rifle platoon had 45 men organized in a grenade discharger section and three rifle sections of 11 men each. The IJN delivered its paratroopers using Mitsubushi Type 96 "Tina" and Kawasaki Type 1 "Thalia" transports.

Yokosuka 1st & 3rd Special Naval Landing Forces
SNLF HQ
HQ Company:
    Company HQ
    Intendance unit
    Signal unit
    Transport unit
    Demolition unit
    Medical unit
    Repair unit
    Command platoon
1st, 2nd & 3rd rifle companies, each:
    Company HQ
    3 rifle platoons (3× LMGs, 4× grenade dischargers)
    HMG platoon (2× HMGs)
    AT unit (2× 3.7cm AT guns)

WEAPONS & EQUIPMENT

Small arms

For the most part Japanese paratroopers used standard infantry weapons, but a number of small arms were modified for their use, with folding stocks or the capability to be 'taken down' into two sections for

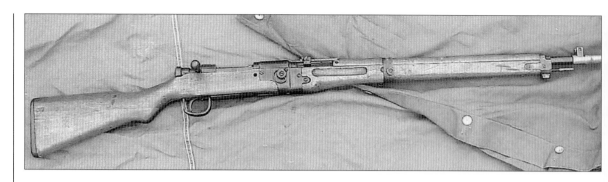

The Arisaka 7.7mm Type 2 (1942) "take-down" rifle, issued from 1943; note the brass muzzle cover. Most Type 2s had a monopod fitted to the forearm, but it has been removed from this example. The unsatisfactory Type 100, which the Type 2 replaced, had lacked the prominent locking pin on the right side of the stock, and the breech portion extending from the barrel was polished. Both rifles were 44in long and weighed just over 8lb 9oz; all Japanese bolt-action rifles had 5-round fixed magazines. (George Kudszus)

the jump. It should be noted, however, that these modified weapons were not available before 1943.

Prior to 1943 IJA paratroopers used the Arisaka 7.7mm Type 99 (1939) short rifle and Nambu 7.7mm Type 99 (1939) light machine gun. IJN paratroopers initially used the Arisaka 6.5mm Meiji Type 38 (1905) carbine and, for ammunition compatibility, the Nambu 6.5mm Type 96 (1936) light machine gun. Since individual weapons were initially dropped separately in cargo containers the Japanese followed the German example and armed all paratroopers with pistols and grenades: 8mm Type 94 (1934) or Nambu Taisho Type 14 (1925) pistols, Meiji Type 30 (1897) bayonets, and two or more HE grenades – a range of WP and other smoke and tear gas grenades were also available. The early operations demonstrated that it was essential for paratroopers to jump with their primary weapons. **Details of small arms are given in the commentaries to Plates C & G at the end of this book.** Glider units used the standard Type 99 (1939) short rifle. Paratroopers also used numerous types of demolition charges, and Type 100 (1940) and Type 3 (1943) flamethrowers were issued to engineers.

A "Japanese paratrooper" – actually, a Japanese-American Nisei – models the jump pack for the disassembled Type 100 sub-machine gun. It is attached to the harness D-rings intended for the chest reserve pack, which was judged unnecessary for low-altitude combat jumps.

Vehicles

Raiding units were provided with small numbers of the Type 95 (1935) light truck, also referred to as a scout car. This was a jeep-like 4×4 vehicle, the truck version of the 1935 *Kurogane* passenger car built by Nihon Nainenki. Actually introduced in 1937, the 1-ton Type 95 could carry a ½-ton load and two men including the driver, at a top road speed of 45mph. Transportable in the Ku-8 glider, it provided infantry elements with some mobility, hauled supplies, towed light guns, and served as a utility and scout vehicle.

When organized in 1944, the 1st Raiding Tank Unit was equipped with 14x Type 2 (1942) *Ke-To* light tanks. The Type 2 was designed in 1941

Crew-served infantry weapons were already designed to be broken down into several packhorse loads, so were suitable for separating into parachute loads and subsequent man-packing; e.g., the 7cm Type 92 infantry gun could be broken down into a half-dozen loads. Most Japanese units were armed with proportionately fewer crew-served weapons than comparable Allied units; parachute units had even fewer, both because of their types of operations and the need to limit heavy equipment in order to be air deployable.

Type 92 HMG
caliber 7.7mm; weight 122lb; feed, 30-rd strip; rate of fire, 400–500rpm
Type 89 grenade discharger
5cm; 10lb 5oz; max range, 710yds (mortar shells), 210yds (Type 91 grenades); ammo – HE, WP, signal
Type 97 AT rifle
2cm; 120lb; 2,000yds; AP-Tracer, HE-Tracer
Type 98 machine cannon
2cm; 836lb; 5,450yds; AP-T, HE-T
Type 94 AT gun
3.7cm; 714lb; 5,000yds; AP, HE
Type 1 AT gun
4.7cm; 1,600lb; 3,000yds; AP, HE
Type 11 infantry gun
3.7cm; 205lb; 2,625yds; AP, HE
Type 92 infantry gun
7cm; 468lb; 3,075yds; AP, HE, WP
Type 94 mountain gun
7.5cm; 1,200lb; 8,750yds; AP, HE, shrapnel, star
Type 97 trench mortar
8cm; 145lb; 3,100yds; HE

as an improvement of the Type 98 (1938); only 29 examples were built. It differed from the Type 98 in having a cylindrical turret providing additional crew space, and a higher velocity 3.7cm Type 1 (1941) gun, plus a 7.7mm Type 97 coaxial machine gun; it carried 93 rounds of 3.7cm and 3,160 of 7.7mm ammunition. At just under 8 tons, it had a top road speed of 30mph, a three-man crew, and 10–16mm armor.

The 1st Raiding Tank Unit's antitank company was provided with 12× Type 94 (1934) tankettes to tow four 4.7cm Type 1 AT guns, and to haul ammunition in $^3/_4$-ton Type 94 full-tracked trailers. The 2.65-ton tankette – almost worthless as a combat vehicle – was armed with a 7.7mm Type 97 MG and manned by a two-man crew protected by 4–12mm armor; top speed was 26mph.

Parachutes

The trials units initially used aircrew emergency parachutes. The **Type 92 (1932)** back-pack parachute was tested first; it required the jumper to pull a ripcord rather than opening automatically by means of a static line, and this resulted in accidental deaths. It was provided with a chest-mounted reserve pack, but not with adequate attachments for equipment. The **Type 97 (1937)** seat-pack ripcord parachute was also tested. Both of these had 24ft-diameter canopies – too small to support a paratrooper and his equipment safely.

The **Type 1 (1941)** parachute was developed specifically for paratroopers and was used by both the IJA and IJN with minor differences. This static line-operated back-pack had a harness based on the British X-type quick release box, with four attaching straps fastened to a junction box over the chest. To release the harness a metal disc on the box was twisted a quarter turn and struck with the hand; this released three of the straps, allowing the jumper to throw off the harness quickly. The Type 1 had two-point riser connections, i.e. two pairs of web straps that fastened the canopy suspension lines permanently to the harness at the shoulders. The **IJN Type 1 Special** was a later model, and was never used in an operational jump. It differed in having a German-style single-point attachment – the suspension lines were all fastened to a large V-ring between the jumper's shoulders. The IJA and IJN Type 1s and the later IJA Type 4 had 5.2m (17ft) static lines, while the IJN Type 1 Special had a 26m (85ft) line – considerably longer than on Western parachutes. Reserve parachutes were seldom used on operational jumps, and weapons or equipment packs were attached to the chest instead.

In 1943 the IJA began development of the **Type 4 (1944)** (referred to in some sources as the "Type 3"). This rig used essentially the same harness, back-pack and single-point attachment as the Type 1 Special, the difference being an inner bag containing the parachute. When opening, the inner bag was pulled from the back-pack by the static line; this "canopy last" design, as also seen in the contemporary British pack, allowed the canopy to inflate with less of an opening shock, and also prevented the deploying canopy and lines from tangling around the body. Additional D-rings were provided on the harness to attach

A blurred but rare photograph of the Type 2 (1942) *Ke-To* tank, of which 14 were provided to the 1st Tank Raiding Unit when it was formed in 1944; it seems to be painted in a three-color camouflage scheme. Only 29 of these tanks were built in total.

Landing with the Type 1 (1941) parachute, with two-point suspension to double webbing risers from the shoulders of the harness. This IJA paratrooper wears the rubber helmet and one-piece jump suit complete with rank patches on the collar, as well as the high-top jump boots more usually associated with the Navy parachute units. Despite the separate development and deployment of Army and Navy units, photos suggest a certain amount of common use of a few equipment items – e.g. see the IJA smocks worn by IJN trainees in the photo on page 5. (Yadao Nakata Collection)

equipment. Both the Type 1 and Type 4 main canopies were 8.5m (28ft) in diameter, and the chest-mounted reserve 7.3m (24ft); the main had 24 panels and suspension lines, the reserve 20. The Type 4's canopy skirt had cambered panels to help reduce oscillation.

Cargo containers

The IJA began conducting parachute cargo drops in 1935; parachutes for 30, 50 & 100kg (66, 110 & 220lb) loads were produced, with cheap cotton canopies. Colored canopies were available to identify the types of loads they carried, though often only white were used. Containers were made of aluminum, wood and canvas, with the parachute pack attached to the top end and a canvas-covered cushion on the bottom. The containers were attached to the external racks of bomber aircraft.

During their initial operations in 1942 both IJA and IJN paratroopers dropped their individual and crew-served weapons, ammunition, light equipment, rations and medical supplies in cargo containers; it was not until 1943 that they were able to jump in carrying their primary weapons.

Individual equipment and uniforms

IJA paratroopers wore standard olive drab cotton or wool field uniforms, and short boots (slightly higher-topped than standard marching shoes) with puttees. A rubber helmet covered with tan brown or olive green cloth was worn for training, and a steel equivalent for combat; a cloth side-and-neck piece had an integral chinstrap and small ear holes. Standard field caps were worn for ground duty. In the early days paratroopers in training wore standard flight coveralls or a one-piece tan jump suit. A light olive green jump smock was later worn over individual equipment, to prevent it from entangling the suspension lines, and to offer some protection during tree landings. The smock had long sleeves and knee-length legs; the front opening and legs fastened by snap closures, allowing rapid removal.

An IJA paratrooper typically wore a standard leather service belt with one or two 30-round leather cartridge boxes on the front, and sometimes a 60-round reserve box centered on the back. The pistol holster was attached to the side or in place of one of the cartridge boxes. The bayonet was worn on the left side, a ration haversack on the left hip, and over this a canteen slung from the shoulder with its strap running under the waist belt. Strapped around the lower torso paratroopers also wore the Type 1 leather-reinforced web bandoleer with seven rifle ammunition and two grenade pockets. Men armed with sub-machine guns had one or

IJA paratrooper manning a standard issue 7.7mm Type 99 light machine gun. He apparently wears the rubber training helmet with segmented cloth cover and broad brow band, and – over his jump smock or jump suit – a short camouflage cape of woven vegetation.

two canvas pouches holding four 30-round magazines. Light machine gun crews carried the various standard pouches and cases for magazines and accessories. The two-man teams with 5cm grenade dischargers each carried two four-pocket pouches for its projectiles.

Other items carried varied between individuals and over time, but might typically include special rations, a small first aid kit, a length of rope, chopsticks, a spare undershirt and socks. Officers additionally carried 6× or 7× binoculars, a leather map case, flashlight and sword. Sometimes a leather service belt was fitted with extra canvas pouches for grenades and pistol magazines and a pistol holster. Besides the special rations, standard packaged and tinned field rations were also used by paratroopers[1]. In addition to the standard 2½-pint canteen, men sometimes carried "water sausages" made of tough cellophane-like material and knotted at short lengths into water-filled sections; each section was bitten through in order to drink the water.

IJN paratroopers wore a special two-piece olive green 50/50 cotton/silk jump uniform. The hip-length jacket was found in two versions, with differing pocket layouts. Bellows front cargo and hip pockets were provided on the trousers, and some had multiple pockets. A lightweight cap similar to the standard field cap was provided with a cloth side-and-neck piece with a chinstrap. An olive drab steel jump helmet was worn over this, with its own chin tapes. High-top brown leather laced jump boots were used, as were unlined brown leather gloves.

---

[1] See also Warrior 95, *Japanese Infantryman 1937–45*. The *Netsuryo Shoku* was issued to paratroopers, aircrew and tank crews for a quick-energy snack; this was a 1½oz paper-wrapped high nutrition bar made of flour, sugar, tea, milk, eggs and butter. The *Assaku Koryo* was a one-day compressed ration wrapped in heavy brown crepe paper, measuring 3⅞in × 3⅛in × 1¾in and weighing 9oz. It included six rectangular cakes of compressed wheat or barley, four cakes of sugar, three brown cakes of dried fish, and one or two pink cakes of salted dried plums. The cakes could be eaten cold, or crumbled into water and cooked as a hot cereal.

IJN paratrooper wearing the steel helmet and dark olive green two-piece jump suit, but here with high puttees and ankle boots. A petty officer's rating patch in red on dark blue can just be made out on his upper right sleeve. He is armed with the Arisaka 6.5mm Meiji Type 38 (1905) carbine – 34.2in long and weighing 7lb 5oz; the long Type 30 (1897) bayonet is fixed. He carries two 17-pocket ammunition bandoleers crossed high on his chest; the small white packet hanging round his neck on a tape contains the ashes of a dead comrade. (Tadao Nakata Collection)

IJN paratroopers at Manado (see below, "Airborne Operations 1942") carried a Type 94 pistol, bayonet, steel helmet, grenades, canteen, haversack with rations, two crossed 17-pocket bandoleers with ammunition for the Type 38 carbine, semaphore flags, small shovel, national flag for air-to-ground recognition, mosquito net and gloves, and a Model 2 first aid kit. Officers carried the same items plus a sword (with a special release strap that allowed it to be lowered on a short cord during the jump), binoculars, flashlight and map case.

AIRBORNE OPERATIONS, 1942

Japanese forces completed only four parachute assaults during the war. The first was conducted by the IJN at Manado, Celebes Island, in the Netherlands East Indies (today, Indonesia) in January 1942, and another at Koepang, West Timor, in February. Army paratroopers made an assault at Palembang, Sumatra, NEI, in February 1942. The final IJA parachute operation was conducted on Leyte in December 1944; and IJA parachute troops executed one last operation in the form of an air-landed raid on Okinawa in April 1945.

THE YOKOSUKA 1st SNLF AT MANADO, JANUARY 1942

After the Yokosuka 1st & 3rd SNLFs had completed training they undertook final exercises on Formosa. The Yokosuka 1st SNLF moved to recently-secured Davao on Mindanao, Philippine Islands, at the end of December

Aircraft used by airborne units
Type & Allied codename – capacity (aircrew/troops)
IJA transports:
Nakajima Ki-34 Type 97 "Thora" – 3/8
Kawasaki Ki-56 Type 1 "Thalia" – 4/14
Mitsubishi Ki-57 Type 100 "Topsy" – 4/15
Nakajima L2D2 Showa Type 0 "Tabby" – 3/21
IJA bombers:
Mitsubishi Ki-21 Type 97 "Sally" – 5/12
Nakajima Ki-49 Type 100 "Helen" – 5/n.a.
IJA gliders:
Kokusai Ku-8 Type 4 "Gander" – 2/24
Kokusai Ku-7 (experimental) – 2/40
IJN transports:
Mitsubishi G3M Type 96 "Tina" – 3/12
Mitsubishi G6M1-L2 Type 1* – 5/20
IJN bomber:
Mitsubishi G4M Type 1 "Betty" – 5/n.a.
(* transport model of G4M Type 1 "Betty")
Most airborne operations were conducted within the operational radius of the available aircraft and *en route* refueling stops were seldom required; ranges to objectives varied from 270 to 440 miles.

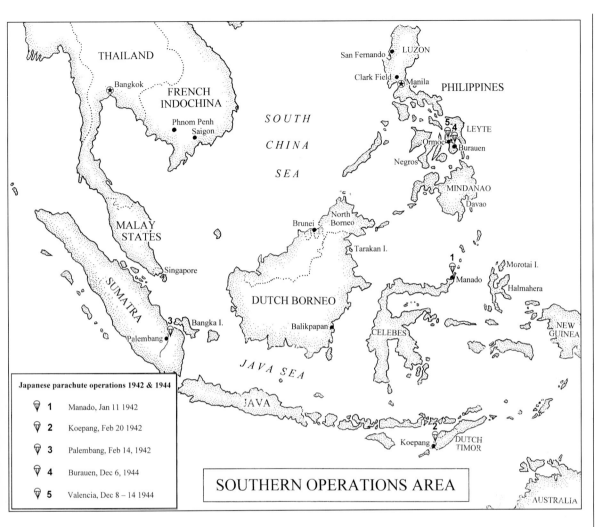

THAILAND

● Bangkok

FRENCH
INDOCHINA

Phnom Penh ●
Saigon ●

S O U T H

C H I N A

S E A

San Fernando ● LUZON

Clark Field ● ★ Manila

PHILIPPINES

5 ▲ **4** LEYTE
Ormoc ● ● Burauen

Negros ●

MINDANAO

● Davao

MALAY
STATES

● Singapore

SUMATRA

Brunei ● North Borneo

● Tarakan I.

3 Bangka I.
Palembang ● ● Bangka I.

DUTCH BORNEO

Balikpapan ●

CELEBES

● Manado **1**

Morotai I.

Halmahera

NEW
GUINEA

J A V A   S E A

JAVA

Japanese parachute operations 1942 & 1944

▽ **1**   Manado, Jan 11 1942

▽ **2**   Koepang, Feb 20 1942

▽ **3**   Palembang, Feb 14, 1942

▽ **4**   Burauen, Dec 6, 1944

▽ **5**   Valencia, Dec 8 – 14 1944

Koepang ● **2** DUTCH
TIMOR

AUSTRALIA

SOUTHERN OPERATIONS AREA

1941. A planned operation to capture oilfields at Tarakan Island off the east coast of Dutch Borneo was canceled when the airfield on Jolo Island could not be readied in time; so Manado was selected as the first IJN parachute objective.

Manado is near the tip of the Minahassa Peninsula in northern Celebes. On January 11, 1942, the Sasebo 1st SNLF would land on the coast of the peninsula on both sides of Manado town, occupy it, and advance toward Kakas the next day. The Sasebo 2nd SNLF would land at Kema on the southeast side of the peninsula and advance to Kakas and Lake Tondano; a cross-peninsula road connects Kema and Manado, and a company of Type 95 light tanks would accompany the amphibious force. This seaborne Sasebo Combined Landing Force (2,500 troops under Capt Kunizo Mori) would attack the enemy at Langoan, cooperating with the Yokosuka 1st SNLF parachuted at Langoan airfield (Manado II) outside Manado town.

The area was defended by Troop Command Manado – 1,500 Dutch troops under Maj B.F.A.Schilmöller, in ten companies mostly of reservists, home guardsmen and native militia. A 45-man Mobile Column with three armored cars was tasked as a reaction force in the event paratroopers were dropped (the type of armored cars is unclear,

Formation of Type 96 "Tina" transports dropping men of the Yokosuka 1st SNLF over Langoan airfield, Manado, Celebes, in January 1942 – Japan's first airborne assault. This is probably the second drop, by 3rd Co, on January 12. The V-formation is typical.

Langoan airfield, January 11 or 12, 1942: because of the short grass the paratroopers had little difficulty recovering their weapons containers, but the lack of cover led to casualties on the DZ.

but those most often employed were Overvalwagen – trucks jury-rigged with armor plate and machine guns.)

The Yokosuka 1st SNLF would fly south some 380 miles from Davao, and would jump over Langoan at 0930hrs on January 11 to seize the airfield and destroy Allied aircraft. While the 1st Co attacked Langoan the 2nd would capture the seaplane base at Kakas. The *1st Drop Group* of 334 men consisted of:

SNLF HQ (44 men – Cdr Horiuchi)
Signal Unit (14 men)
1st Co (139 men – Lt(jg) Mutaguchi)
2nd Co (137 men – Lt(jg) Saito)

The *2nd Drop Group*, comprising 3rd Co (74 men – Lt(jg) Sonobe), would jump on to Langoan airfield as reinforcements on January 12. The Lake Tondano Landing Group of 22 men would depart Davao on

Langoan airfield – the lack of urgency in this scene suggests that it too shows the aftermath of the 3rd Co drop on January 12. The paratroopers have assembled by sections, and canopies and cargo containers lie discarded in the background. The IJN paratrooper at right foreground can be seen to have a Type 38 carbine and crossed bandoleers.

January 11 aboard two four-engine Kawanishi H6K5 Type 97 "Mavis" flying boats, to land on the lake. This party comprised the AT gun unit (10 men, 1× 3.7cm AT gun) and medical section (11 men).

The Type 96 "Tina" transports of the 1st Drop Group would fly with an interval of 1,500m between each company, with ten aircraft in the 1st and 2nd Cos and eight in the 3rd. Each transport carried 12 paratroopers, five cargo containers beneath the plane and two containers inside. The drop would be from an altitude of 500ft at a speed of 100 knots.

The amphibious landing force departed Davao on January 9; the Sasebo 2nd SNLF landed at Kema at 0300hrs on January 11, and the Sasebo 1st SNLF at Manado town at 0400 hours. At 0630 the 28 transports took off from Davao airfield. As they approached Celebes a Japanese seaplane mistakenly shot down one transport, with the loss of all aboard.

At 0952 the formation came over the objective, and the drop was completed at 1020 hours. As they dropped, Dutch defenders under 1st Lt J.G.Wielimnga opened fire and the paratroopers suffered several casualties. Some landed close to enemy pillboxes, which they attacked and destroyed; this allowed paratroopers who were pinned down on the airfield drop zone to move out, and their subsequent attacks on the remaining Dutch positions turned the tide of the action. One Dutch armored car came from the direction of Kakas and fired on the paratroopers, but was captured; later the other two attacked, but one was knocked out and the other driven off.

At 1125 the Japanese secured the airfield and then advanced on Kakas; there they defeated some 150 enemy troops equipped with an armored car and an AT gun, capturing the base at 1450 hours. The two flying boats landed on Lake Tondano at 1457, and the AT unit and medics linked up with the paratroopers.

The next day at 0630hrs the 2nd Drop Group jumped from 18 transports over Langoan airfield, and the reinforced paratroopers swept into the town, from which the Dutch had already retreated. The paratroopers soon linked up with elements of the seaborne force. The two-day fight had cost the Yokosuka 1st SNLF 20 dead (plus the 12 lost aboard the downed transport) and 32 wounded. They killed some 140 Dutch troops and captured 48 others.

Cdr Toyaki Horiuchi, commanding officer of the Yokosuka 1st SNLF, in a posed photo – note his shirt collar and necktie, and sleeve rank insignia (in gold on light brown). Although he was 40 years old at the time of the Manado jump, he was a renowned athlete who had introduced Swedish gymnastics to the IJN training program. In September 1948, Horiuchi was executed for atrocities committed at Manado. (Tadao Nakata Collection)

THE YOKOSUKA 3rd SNLF AT KOEPANG, FEBRUARY 1942

In early January 1942 the Yokosuka 3rd SNLF moved from Formosa to Tarakan Island. An initial plan to drop the unit at Balikpapan, an oil refinery on Borneo's east coast, was canceled. At the end of January they moved to Kendari, southeast Celebes, for the Koepang drop. Koepang (today spelt Kupang) was the capital of Dutch or West Timor, situated near the island's southwest tip. The objective was Penfui airfield, about 7 miles southeast of the town, an important staging base for aircraft deploying from Australia for the defense of Java. Because the paratroopers who dropped directly on Manado airfield had suffered heavy casualties, a DZ was selected on the plain near Babau, about 10½ miles northeast of the airfield. The area was defended by an Australian and Dutch force, with the Combined Defence Headquarters at Penfui airfield under command of Australian Brig W.C.D.Veale. The 1,000-man Australian 2/40th Inf Bn defended the beaches northeast of Koepang and the airfield itself, where a 40mm AA troop and C Co, 2/40th Infantry were located. The 600-strong Dutch Timor Garrison Bn defended beaches to the west of the town. 2/40th Battalion's reserve was D Co, at Koepang, and the battalion support echelon was at Babau near the Japanese drop zone. The Royal Australian Air Force squadron at Penfui had already been withdrawn.

The Yokosuka 3rd SNLF loaded aboard 28 "Tina" and "Thalia" transports at Kendari airfield early on February 20. At 0600 they took off, together with 17 Type 1 "Betty" bombers, for the 420-mile flight – the longest range Japanese parachute operation. The *1st Drop Group* had 308 men:

SNLF HQ (Lt Cdr Fukumi)
1st Co (Lt(jg) Yamabe)
3rd Co (Ens Miyamoto)

The *2nd Drop Group* (323 men of 2nd Co, under Lt(jg) Sakurada, and support elements) would jump in on February 21.

The operation

In the early morning of the 20th, 4,600 troops of the Ito Detachment (reinforced 228th Inf Regt detached from the 38th Div, and Kure 1st SNLF) landed unopposed behind the defenders, on the south side of the island. The Left and Center Attack Groups would move north to Koepang, and the Kure 1st SNLF from the Center Attack Group would split off to relieve the paratroopers who had secured the airfield; the Right Attack Group would move northeast toward Usua, a few kilometers east of Babau. Unexpectedly, the Allied beach defenders withdrew eastwards.

The "Bettys" bombed the DZ before the paratroopers jumped at 1000hrs, meeting no opposition. They had assembled by 1045, and at 1130 they moved south to Babau and the road to Koepang. There they encountered troops of the 2/40th Bn's rear echelon formed into an *ad hoc* defense force, and from 1300 the paratroopers of 1st Co were heavily engaged. Prisoner interrogation and a cloud of dust in the direction of Koepang indicated that a larger force was approaching; this was D Co, accompanied by Dutch tankettes and armored cars, which had been ordered to Babau when paratroop drops were reported. D Company counter-attacked at 1430; the paratroopers were engaged

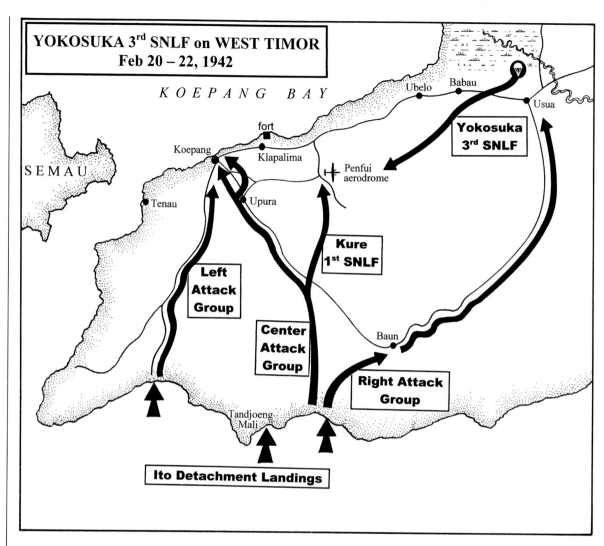

YOKOSUKA 3rd SNLF on WEST TIMOR
Feb 20 – 22, 1942

KOEPANG BAY

SEMAU

Tenau

Koepang

fort

Klapalima

Upura

Penfui aerodrome

Ubelo   Babau

Usua

Yokosuka 3rd SNLF

Kure 1st SNLF

Left Attack Group

Center Attack Group

Right Attack Group

Baun

Tandjoeng Mali

Ito Detachment Landings

in hand-to-hand combat until the enemy withdrew at sunset, D Co west to Ubelo and the Babau defenders east to Usua. During this fight 22 Japanese were killed and 30 wounded.

To bypass the Allied troops, Cdr Fukumi decided to leave the road at about 2200hrs and march southwest through the jungle to Penfui airfield; he strove to avoid engagements *en route*, so that the capture of his objective would not be delayed. However, the jungle was extremely dense and the night-long march, carrying the wounded, was very difficult. In the early morning they reached a hill that gave some visibility.

The 26 transports of the 2nd Drop Group took off from Kendari at 0600hrs on February 21, and at 1000 dropped them at the same DZ as the 1st Group. From their hill the 1st Group observed this drop; Cdr Fukumi feared that if they advanced down the road 2nd Co would run into the enemy as he had done, so he sent a messenger to the 2nd Drop Group telling them to move through the jungle. Advancing to Babau, this second lift were attacked in their turn by D Co of the 2/40th, losing 14 dead and four wounded. After repulsing the Australians the paratroopers entered the jungle led by Cdr Fukimi's guide.

Probably photographed during an exercise – note the thick brow pad around the helmets – these IJN paratroopers are heavily burdened with weapons, ammunition and equipment bags. The Navy *Gunkanki* rising sun ensign is being used as an assembly aid and for air/ground recognition.

The 1st Drop Group continued to struggle through the forest, reaching Penfui on the morning of the 22nd, only to find that the airfield had already been occupied by the Kure 1st SNLF the day before. Allied forces still in the area surrendered on the 23rd.

Later service

After the Philippines, Malaya, the Dutch East Indies and the Solomons had been secured, the IJN planned further conquests; they had more distant goals than the Army. The IJN intended to seize Port Moresby on the south coast of New Guinea in May 1942, Midway and the western Aleutian Islands in June, New Caledonia in July, and Fiji and Samoa in August. Future plans were even more ambitious, with proposals to invade Hawaii, northern Australia and Ceylon. In the event the IJN's catastrophic losses of ships and aircraft in the June 1942 battle of Midway brought a halt to Japanese conquests, and the IJN parachute units were disbanded.

The Yokosuka 1st and 3rd SNLFs returned to Japan in December 1942, and were consolidated into the Yokosuka 1st SNLF – no longer a parachute unit, but a conventional seaborne force. In June 1943, a new Yokosuka 2nd SNLF was organized (the original unit had been disbanded after its operations in British Borneo) from 1st SNLF personnel, and was sent to Nauru Island west of the Gilberts, where it spent the rest of the war. In September 1943 the 900-man Yokosuka 1st SNLF deployed to Saipan; a 200-man detachment was sent to Rabaul, New Britain, but were diverted to Truk where they remained until the Japanese surrender. The force on Saipan was destroyed while resisting the US Marine landings in June 1944.

THE 2nd RAIDING REGIMENT AT PALEMBANG, FEBRUARY 1942

In September 1940 – before the IJA parachute troops existed – an IGHQ planning group had studied a possible operation against Palembang, the capital of Sumatra, Netherlands East Indies, where two large oil refineries were situated. Palembang is 50 miles inland from the northeast coast; it was essential that the refineries be captured intact, yet an amphibious force approaching up the Musi River would allow the Dutch enough warning to destroy them.

In August 1941 an airborne operation against Palembang was included in plans for the conquest of Southeast Asia, although the IGHQ was concerned that the paratroop units would not be operational in time. However, on October 28 the first successful demonstration by the IJA paratroopers was mounted at Takanabe for senior staff, and it was quickly decided to commit them at Palembang.

On December 1 the 1st Raiding Bde was mobilized, but their objective and target date were withheld for security reasons until after the Pacific War began on the 7th; maps and aerial photos of Palembang were then passed to the brigade headquarters. The brigade was attached to the Southern Army (Gen Count Hisaichi Terauchi); the Palembang mission was designated the "L Operation", under 16th Army (LtGen Hitoshi Imamura.) Initially the 1st Raiding Regt was scheduled to drop at Palembang, and on December 19 it departed Japan aboard the transport *Meiko Maru*. On January 3, 1942, the ship was in the South China Sea bound for Indochina when it suddenly caught fire, later sinking off Hainan Island. (Various sources blame spontaneous combustion of ammunition, or an accidental gasoline fire.) Escort vessels rescued the paratroopers, but they lost all of their equipment and were exhausted.

February 14, 1942: paratroopers of the 2nd Raiding Regt don their Type 1 parachutes on Keluang airfield in Malaya for the Palembang operation. They have not yet snapped their smock legs tightly around the thighs. Note the parachute carrying cases at their feet.

At short notice the 2nd Raiding Regt was given the mission. The regiment was still being organized, but hurriedly completed its formation and drew weapons and parachutes. On January 15 the unit left Japan, arriving at Phnom Penh, Cambodia, on February 2. The air units for the drop also arrived: the Raiding Flying Regt, 98th Flying Regt, and 12th Transport Company. At Phnom Penh the paratroopers checked and packed their parachutes and loaded rifles, machine guns, ammunition and supplies into cargo containers; their own bombers were unavailable to drop these, and they had to be entrusted to other units. Coordinating the cargo drops in both time and location was critical, especially as different units were dropping the troops and the containers. If the latter were misdropped or delayed, the paratroopers on the ground would be forced to fight a well-armed enemy with only pistols and grenades.

The force was assembled at Sungai Petani in Malaya on February 11. On the 13th the *1st Attack Group* moved to Keluang and Kahang airfields in southern Malaya, while the *2nd Attack Group* remained at Sungai Petani. Keluang housed the Raiding Bde HQ, 2nd Raiding Regt (–) with 330 men, Raiding Flying Regt, 12th Transport Co & 64th Flying Regt; at Kahang were the 98th, 90th & 59th Flying Regts, and scout elements of the 15th Independent Flying Unit & 81st Flying Regiment. Lieutenant-General Michio Sugawara, commander of the 3rd Air Group, visited Keluang to encourage the men and give final orders. He served *sake* and *sushi* to the paratroopers, announcing, "This is your last taste of Japan. Drink and eat fully, without ceremony." The paratroopers poured each other drinks and enjoyed the delicacies of this "last supper."

The plan

There were two primary objectives: Pangkalanbenteng airfield (called Aerodrome P1 by the British) 8 miles north of the town, and the two refineries along the south bank of the Musi River which flowed through it. From a military viewpoint the airfield was the primary target, but the refineries had considerable economic importance. Southern Army did not think that the paratroopers had sufficient strength to occupy the airfield and refineries simultaneously, and were forced to risk giving priority to the airfield, since this would provide a base of operations and a means of delivering supplies. From there the paratroopers would have to hasten to the Musi River, which was spanned by few bridges, and secure both refineries – which themselves were separated by the Komering River, a tributary of the Musi. The east refinery was operated by the Nederlandsche Koloniale Petroleum Maatschappij (NKPM) and the larger west refinery by the Bataafsche Petroleum Maatschappij (BPM); the latter was divided between two separate compounds. Aerodrome P1 was occupied by two Allied fighter squadrons. The area's defenses were under the Dutch LtCol L.N.W.Vogelesang with some 2,000 troops of Territorial Command South Sumatra; these included the South Sumatra Garrison Bn of Dutch regulars at P1 and a reserve company at Palembang, plus eight 75mm guns. Small regular detachments defended the refineries, and a few armored cars were available to the defenders. Part of the British 6th Heavy AA Regt, Royal Artillery, deployed six each 3.7in and 40mm guns at the airfield and a further four of each caliber at the refineries. There were also some

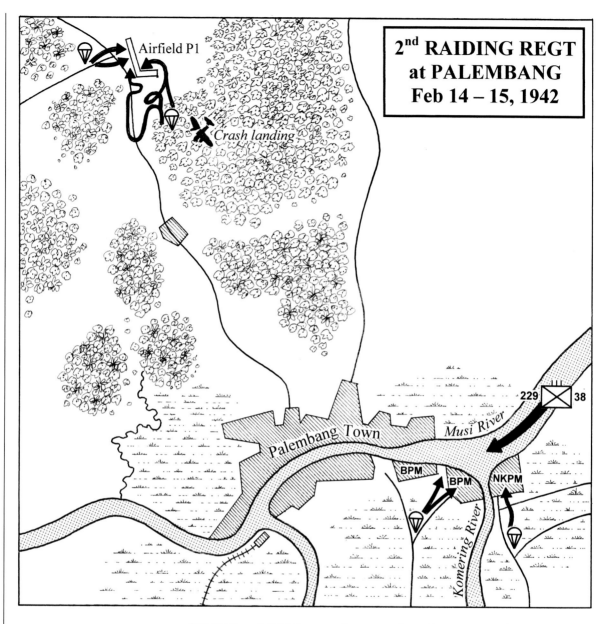

2nd **RAIDING REGT at PALEMBANG Feb 14 – 15, 1942**

Crash landing

Airfield P1

Palembang Town

Musi River

Komering River

229 | 38

BPM

BPM

NKPM

260 RAF and RAAF ground crew and service personnel at P1, though lacking adequate infantry weapons or combat training.

It was planned that the main body of paratroopers would drop just southeast and west of the airfield, and two small groups just outside the refineries. On February 11 the 1st Raiding Bde issued orders detailing the attack plan in two phases, on L-1 Day and L-Day respectively. On L-1, February 14, a battalion of Col Tanaka's reinforced 229th Inf Regt from the 38th Div would secure Bangka Island off the coast, and the first parachute drops would also take place. On L-Day the rest of the 229th Infantry would move up the Musi River to Palembang in landing barges. They anticipated reaching the town only on L+2; until this relief arrived the paratroopers would have to hold their objectives alone. The 2nd Raiding Regt's organization and drop zones were as follows:

1st Attack Group
1,200m SE of airfield P1 (180 men):
    Regt HQ (17 men – Maj Komura)
    Signal Unit (30 men – Lt Komaki)
    4th Co (97 men – Lt Mitsuya)
    3rd Plt, 2nd Co (36 men – Lt Mizuno)
200m W of airfield:
    2nd Co (-) (60 men – Lt Hirose)
500m W of refineries:
    1st Co (-) (60 men – Lt Nakao)
700m S of refineries:
    3rd Plt, 1st Co (39 men – Lt Hasebe)

The Raiding Flying Regt and attached 3rd Air Group units would transport the paratroopers and provide escort:
Raiding Flying Regt (Maj Niihara):
1st Co (12x Type 1 transports) & 3rd Co (12× Type 100) –
    18× transports SE of airfield, 6× W of airfield
2nd Co (9× Type 1) – 6× W of refineries, 3× S of refineries
98th Flying Regt (cargo drop):
    15× Type 97 bombers SE of airfield, 3× W of airfield,
    6× W of refineries, 3× S of refineries
64th Flying Regt (escort to airfield)
    3 cos Ki-43 Type 1 "Oscar" fighters
59th Flying Regt (escort to refineries)
    2 cos Type 1 fighters
90th Flying Regt (air support)
    1 co, 9× Type 99 light bombers

2nd Attack Group (airfield, second lift):
3rd Co, 2nd Raiding Regt (90 men – Lt Morisawa)
    12th Transport Co (Type 1 transports)
    1 co, 98th Flying Regt (cargo drop)
    9× Type 97 bombers
    Elements, 59th & 64th Flying Regts (Type 1 fighters)

Upon the landing of the 1st Attack Group, the 1st Raiding Bde commander, Col Kume, and some of his staff planned to ride in on a transport and crash-land between the airfield and Palembang town. The transport would carry a 3.7cm AT gun, which could not be loaded in parachute cargo containers.

L-1: the airfield
The paratroopers were awakened at 0700 hours on February 14 after only two hours' rest. At 0830 all aircraft on both airfields took off, to rendezvous over Batu Pahat northwest of Singapore. Thirty-four transports and 27 bombers assembled in the formation, escorted by 80 Type 1 fighters and nine Type 99 light bombers, with a Type 100 scout plane leading the formation 350 miles southeastwards at an altitude of 9,850 feet. This armada of over 150 aircraft represented Japan's largest airborne operation.

At 1120 hours they arrived over the mouth of the Musi River – partly hidden by the vast smoke cloud drifting from distant burning Singapore

– and separated into two groups. Allied AA fire burst around them, but the transports came in at low altitude without loss and dropped most of the sticks on their assigned DZs; the drop at the airfield took place at 1126 and at the refineries four minutes later. Following the transports, the heavy bombers dropped their cargo containers and strafed the area; one bomber was shot down over the refineries. Fighters of 64th Flying Regt engaged five Hurricanes at 2,600ft over the airfield and shot one down; encountering another ten at 6,500ft, they downed two without loss. Light bombers hit barracks and AA positions at the airfield; since no enemy aircraft were found over the refineries, the "Oscars" of 59th Flying Regt strafed the area.

The 180 paratroopers of the airfield group landed just under 2 miles southeast of the airfield, except for one load. On aerial photographs the terrain appeared to be covered with low bush; in fact it was wooded with small trees, and many cargo containers became snagged in these and were difficult or impossible to recover. The trees also restricted visibility and the paratroopers had difficulty in finding one another. They gradually assembled in small groups as they moved towards the airfield, many still armed only with pistols. British AA guns were firing blind into the DZ, but inflicted no casualties.

The stick led by Lt Okumoto of 4th Co had their jump delayed by a jammed door, and landed near the road between Palembang and the airfield. Here Okumoto and four men encountered four trucks loaded with 40 Dutch soldiers fleeing south, and engaged them with pistols; these soldiers – probably irregulars – surrendered. Around 1200hrs two armored cars and four troop trucks came north from the direction of Palembang; surprised by pistol fire and grenades, some 150 demoralized soldiers abandoned their vehicles, except for an armored car and one

(Continued on page 41)

This oblique view to the northeast shows the broad bend of the Musi River in the background, with the city of Palembang on its far bank to the left; in the left foreground are the large facilities of the Pladjoe (BPM) oil refinery, and beyond, across the tributary Komering River, the Soengai Gerong (NKPM) refinery. Though not of good quality, this photo does give a stark impression of the sheer size of the objectives allocated initially to about 100 men of the 2nd Raiding Regt's first lift.

IMPERIAL JAPANESE ARMY PARATROOPS

1: Paratrooper in training, 1941
2: Paratrooper, 2nd Raiding Regt; Palembang operation, Feb 1942
3: Paratroop officer on operations, 1942
4 & 5: IJA paratrooper insignia

1

3

2

4

5

A

B

2nd **RAIDING REGIMENT AT PALEMBANG, SUMATRA; FEBRUARY 14, 1942**
See text commentary for details

PARATROOPERS' WEAPONS
See text commentary for details

C

IMPERIAL JAPANESE NAVY PARATROOPERS
1: Paratrooper, barracks dress, 1942
2 & 3: Paratrooper on operations, 1942
4: Paratrooper's rating patches

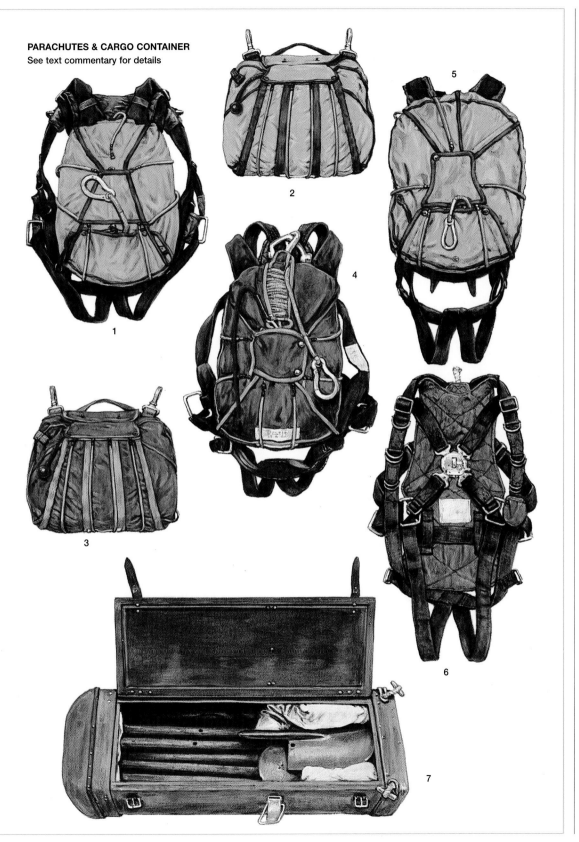

PARACHUTES & CARGO CONTAINER
See text commentary for details

1

2

3

4

5

6

7

E

YOKOSUKA 1st SNLF AT MANADO, CELEBES; JANUARY 11, 1942
See text commentary for details

F

PARATROOPERS' WEAPONS
See text commentary for details

G

IJA AIRBORNE TROOPS, 1944–45

1: Kaoru Airborne Raiding Detachment; Leyte operation, Nov 26, 1944
2: 2nd Raiding Bde; Leyte operation, Dec 6, 1944
3: Giretsu Airborne Unit; Okinawa operation, May 24, 1945
4: Unidentified insignia

truck. During this fight two paratroopers were killed and Lt Okumoto was wounded. Okumoto and his paratroopers had inadvertently established a useful roadblock between Palembang town and the airfield.

Regimental commander Maj Komura, with ten men, was advancing through the trees about a mile southeast of the airfield when, at about 1330, he met the 4th Co commander, Lt Mitsuya, with 24 paratroopers; then Lt Okumoto also reported in, with a captured armored car. Major Komura decided to maintain the roadblock on the Palemberg road, but ordered Lt Mitsuya to advance and seize the airfield office. Mitsuya sent Lt Ooki and 20 men north with the captured armored car; they encountered about 300 Allied troops coming from the airfield. After a fierce fight the paratroopers repulsed the enemy and pursued them back to P1, which they found abandoned; the office was captured at 1820 hours.

Major Komura attempted to assemble other scattered paratroopers, fighting skirmishes in thick cover with fleeing Dutch troops. At 1800 he met Lt Komaki of the Signal Unit at the east end of the airfield, and at 2100 he joined Mitsuya at the buildings. Paratroopers gathered on the airfield, coming in singly and in small groups; they spent the night securing positions, but no counter-attack took place.

Sixty paratroopers of 2nd Co had dropped west of the airfield on what had been thought to be grassland; it was actually covered with dense 6ft reeds, which made it very difficult for them to find one another and almost impossible to locate cargo containers. Regardless, scattered groups advanced east towards P1. Lieutenant Gamo gathered 16 men and pushed on, armed only with pistols and grenades. Suddenly they came upon an AA gun position; Gamo threw a grenade and dashed forwards, but was shot dead. The rest of the men continued towards the airfield.

The 2nd Co commander, Lt Hirose, found only two other paratroopers, but reached the airfield's west barracks at around 1400 hours. Sighting about 350 Dutch troops, he turned back. He found another paratrooper; and when the four men approached the barracks again around 1700hrs they found it deserted. The Japanese were delighted to find food still on the stoves – they had jumped with only minimal compressed rations.

L-1: the refineries

Sixty paratroopers of the 1st Co landed south and west of the BPM refineries, in a shallow marsh whose light vegetation enabled them to find their cargo containers and arm themselves. Platoon commander Lt Tokunaga with six men captured a pillbox in the southwest portion of the refinery. He then advanced north through a residential area, and engaged about 60 Allied soldiers equipped with machine guns. Lieutenants Ogawa and Yosioka soon arrived with small groups, and Tokunaga ordered them to secure the topping installations while he kept the defenders occupied. A dozen paratroopers rushed through the facility, and raised a Rising Sun flag on the central topping tower at some disputed time between 1310 and 1350 hours.

Seeing the flag, Lt Tokunaga and the 1st Co commander, Lt Nakao, moved towards it; as they advanced they closed a boiler's valves and shut down other refinery equipment to avoid damage. The Allied defenders launched a determined counter-attack which led to combat at ranges under 50 yards; bullets punctured pipes, and the spewing oil was set

Officers of the 2nd Raiding Regt, one still wearing his jump helmet, with officers of the relieving 229th Inf Regt, as the NKPM refinery burns in the background. The IJA claimed to have killed some 530 Allied troops and captured 13 AA guns in the vicinity of the airfield, and another 550 at the refineries, with ten more guns, several armored cars and numerous trucks captured – though British ground crews did manage to destroy all the remaining aircraft on P1. The paratroopers lost 29 dead, 37 seriously wounded, and 11 lightly wounded – roughly 12 percent of the troops who jumped (two were killed due to parachute malfunctions.) One Japanese heavy bomber was shot down, and two transports crash-landed – one as planned with the brigade commander, and another due to engine failure.

alight by an Allied mortar round. Nakao ordered Tokunaga's platoon to attack, and they made headway northwards across the refinery, but the fighting continued through the night. Sergeant Kamoshida had jumped last and got separated from his men. He found his way into the refinery's residential area alone, killing defenders with his pistol, but when he reached an office building he was seriously wounded by machine gun fire; after throwing his last grenade he committed suicide with his pistol.

Lieutenant Hasebe's platoon dropped south of the NKPM refinery, into a deep swamp, but used a native boat to recover cargo containers. Two paratroopers had landed directly in front of an Allied position; coming under fire, they attacked with pistols and grenades, killing eight defenders. They advanced up a road to the refinery, but when one was wounded by fire from the buildings they turned back to find their platoon.

The road to the NKPM refinery ran straight through the swamp for 300 yards, devoid of cover and swept by heavy Allied fire. Hasebe could find no flanking route, and was obliged to attack along the road; he got to within 100 yards of the refinery before he was killed and the attack stalled. Sergeant Tanba took over the platoon, and decided to wait until nightfall before trying to work their way forward. At 2300hrs they advanced into the refinery, to find that the defenders had retreated under cover of darkness. At 0600 a delay-fused Dutch demolition charge exploded, and the resulting fire destroyed about 80 percent of the NKPM facility.

L-Day

At 1030 hours on February 15 a scout plane from Keluang landed at airfield P1. Told that many of the cargo containers had not been recovered, the pilot returned to Keluang to report the situation and the known locations of the paratroopers. This was Gen Sugawara's first report of success, since radio contact with the paratroops had not been established. He hurried to send transports with weapons and ammunition containers.

Shortly before noon Col Kume managed to reach the airfield. The previous day he had crash-landed several kilometers southeast of the airfield; crawling through the soggy woodland, he had spent a sleepless night tormented by swarms of mosquitoes. At 1300 hours the second lift arrived: 90 paratroopers of the 3rd Co dropped safely on the airfield as planned, and Col Kume sent a platoon to reconnoiter Palembang town. Lieutenant Adachi's platoon reached Palembang at 1730, and discovered that the city was undefended. They did find two Dutch armored patrol boats on the Musi River, and immobilized one with small arms fire. On receiving Adachi's report Kume ordered the 3rd Co into the city. That evening they made contact with the paratroopers at the refineries. The troops of the 229th Infantry arrived at Palembang by landing barge during the night of February 15, ahead of schedule. On February 20, the 38th Div took over control of Palembang from the paratroopers.

This successful operation was, in the event, the Japanese parachute troops' most significant victory. Although one refinery was seriously damaged, the larger one was captured almost intact. General Terauchi was warmly appreciative of the 1st Raiding Brigade's effectiveness.

Later service

After the Palembang operation the paratroopers returned to Phnom Penh, where the 1st Raiding Regt joined them after its ordeal at sea. After the East Indies campaign the focus of the war shifted to Burma, and on April 8, 1942, the 1st and part of the 2nd Raiding Regt arrived in Rangoon. The Japanese were driving Allied forces out of Burma, and an airborne operation was planned against Lashio on the "Burma Road", the main withdrawal route for the defeated Chinese 66th Army. The timing was problematic, given the rapidly changing situation on the ground. The 15th Army staff, under LtGen Shojiro Iida, at first judged that ground forces would reach Lashio around May 10, so the jump was planned for May 5. However, the Japanese advanced more rapidly than expected; estimating that they would reach Lashio before the end of April, the staff advanced the drop to April 29.

That morning some 70 transports carrying the 1st Raiding Regt took off from Toungoo airfield north of Rangoon, for the 310-mile flight northeast to Lashio. However, as they approached the objective the weather quickly deteriorated, and LtCol Niihara of the 1st Raiding Flying Regt aborted the mission. (At around noon that day, infantry of the 56th Div entered Lashio.)

In July 1942 the IJA paratroops returned to Nyutabaru, Japan. Before the war the existence of their unit was so secret that they could not even tell their families; now they had done their share in conquering the "Southern Resource Zone" the media lauded them as heroic *Sora no Shimpei* – "soldier gods of the sky". Additional raiding units would be raised; but since Japan shifted to the defensive in late 1942, there would be few opportunities to employ assault troops in their planned role. Operations were planned on Eastern New Guinea, and Attu Island in the Aleutians, but these were canceled.

AIRBORNE OPERATIONS, 1944–45

OPERATIONS ON LEYTE
The Kaoru Airborne Raiding Detachment, November 1944
The Kaoru Airborne Raiding Detachment was formed as an element of the Guerrilla Unit *(Yugekitai)*, of which two companies were raised in December 1943, largely recruited from the Takasago tribe on Formosa. The Takasago were famous as courageous and skilled jungle fighters, who traditionally carried a short *giyuto* ("loyalty sword".) Officers and technical soldiers such as medics and signalers were Japanese. Inspired by the success of provisional raider units formed in eastern New Guinea, the *Yugekitai* was trained by the staff of the Nakano intelligence school in guerrilla and infiltration tactics, demolitions, camouflage, and the use of special weapons and equipment. In May 1944 two guerrilla companies were assigned to the 2nd Area Army, responsible for the Netherlands East Indies and headquartered at Manado; and in June they landed at Manila, capital of the Philippines. The 2nd Guerrilla Co moved to Halmahera, but the 1st Co remained on Luzon. (The 2nd Guerrilla Co was later sent to Morotai Island, NEI, after the American landings in September 1944.)

When US forces landed on Leyte in the Philippines on October 20, 1944, the 4th Air Army decided to use the 1st Guerrilla Co for an airborne attack on airfields now in American hands. Under the command of Lt Shigeo Naka, they were quickly trained in air-landing operations; it was planned that transport aircraft carrying guerrillas armed with demolition charges would deliberately make belly landings on the airfields. The unit was named the Kaoru Airborne Raiding Detachment (*Kaoru* means "distinguished service"), and the operation was designated *Gi*. Four transports each with ten raiders aboard were to land on the North and South Burauen airfields in the US beachhead on east central Leyte, to attack parked aircraft and installations.

The unit was alerted on November 22; and on the night of the 26th, four Type 0 "Tabby" transports carrying 40 Kaoru Unit raiders under Lt Naka took off from Lipa airfield south of Manila. Flying at very low altitude to avoid American fighters, they headed for Leyte some 350 miles to the southeast. Two hours after take-off they reported that they were over the target – and that was the last that was heard from them. Next day no American aircraft appeared over Ormoc Bay on the

Men of the Kaoru Airborne Raiding Detachment in the wicker seats of a Type 0 "Tabby" transport during a practice flight. Kneeling in the center, holding his sword (note that his white gloves have been painted black) is Lt Kaku; he wears his field cap under his helmet, and has a chest haversack for demolitions charges, as worn by most of these raiders for their Leyte operation on November 26, 1944. In the foreground note one of the white recognition sashes worn by officers and NCOs for the operation.

west of Leyte, where Japanese convoys were landing reinforcements, so it was assumed that the *Gi* Operation had been successful. In fact, judging from the crash of some aircraft near airfields other than the raid's objectives, it appears that the pilots went astray.

One transport landed in the sea just offshore near Dulag airfield. When an American patrol approached, the occupants threw a grenade; the patrol returned fire, killing two raiders, but the remainder swam ashore and escaped inland. The second plane landed on Bito Beach near Abuyog airfield; US troops killed one raider, and the rest escaped into the jungle. The third plane reached the two Burauen airfields, but was shot down by AA fire and all aboard were killed. The fourth plane missed its course and landed near Ormoc, where the raiders linked up with Japanese troops. The escaped Kaoru raiders may have attempted to carry out independent guerrilla attacks, but are more likely to have joined up with 16th Div troops fighting the invaders; details are unknown.

The 2nd Raiding Brigade, December 1944

During the IJA paratroopers' long rest in Japan, additional units were organized. The 1st & 2nd Training Raiding Regts were disbanded and their personnel assigned to new 3rd & 4th Raiding Regts in August 1944, the 5th Raiding Regt being absorbed into the new 1st & 2nd Glider Infantry Regiments. The 2nd Raiding Bde was activated on November 6 that year under command of Col Kenji Tokunaga; its codename was "Takachiho" (after a town in central Kyushu, with mystical significance in Shinto legends), and the formation were sometimes called the "Takachiho paratroopers."

The US landings on Leyte in October 1944 finally brought the IJA paratroopers back into action; on October 25, IGHQ ordered the forming 2nd Raiding Bde to deploy to the Philippines. The 3rd Raiding Regt (Maj Tsuneharu Shirai) left Japan aboard the aircraft carrier *Junyo* on October 30, avoiding US submarines and aircraft and arriving at Manila, Luzon, on November 11; the 2nd Raiding Bde HQ arrived by

Members of the Kaoru Detachment cheer the Emperor before departing for their attack on the Burauen airfields on Leyte: *"Tenno haika! Banzai, banzai, banzai!"* ("May the Emperor live ten thousand years!"). Officers and NCOs, with white sashes, raise their swords and some enlisted men the *giyuto* knives of the Formosan Takasago tribesmen. Note the white armbands worn by rankers (see Plate H1.)

air the same day. The 4th Raiding Regt (Maj Chisaku Saida) sailed aboard the transport *Akagisan Maru* on November 3, and arrived at San Fernando, Luzon, on November 30. The 2nd Raiding Bde then assembled at Clark Field north of Manila, but their 1st & 2nd Raiding Flying Regts remained on Formosa.

The Burauen raid

The Japanese were willing to make major sacrifices to eject US forces from Leyte, and regardless of the failure of the Kaoru unit they were not deterred from another attempt against US-held airfields. This would be a larger and better coordinated effort as part of a continuing air offensive, and its planning by 14th Area Army on Luzon and 4th Air Army (LtGen Kyoji Tominaga) had begun before the *Gi* Operation was attempted as a stop-gap measure.

Japanese forces on Leyte were under 35th Army (LtGen Sosaku Susuki.) The paratroopers and the 16th Div (LtGen Shiro Makino) were tasked with occupying the three Burauen airfields[2], where the 26th Div (LtGen Tsuyuo Yamagata) was to reinforce them by crossing the mountains eastwards from Ormoc. The airborne operation was codenamed *Te*, and the ground operation *Wa*. Later, airborne attacks against the Dulag and Tacloban airfields were added to the plan by request of the 3rd Raiding Regt commander.

For the *Te* Operation the 3rd Raiding Regt and part of the 4th were divided into three echelons; the detachment targeted on each airfield sometimes included men from both units. Type 100 "Helen" heavy bombers were to crash-land on the airfields; raiders riding in these

2 The Burauen airfields included Burauen North and South, and the smaller San Pablo strip just to the east. The Japanese referred to Burauen North & South as Buri and Bayung respectively.

were to attack the priority targets – parked aircraft and supply dumps – with demolition charges. Other paratroopers would jump from Type 100 "Topsy" transports, to engage US forces and attack AA gun positions and any other facilities they found:

Buri (Burauen South) airfield
204–260 men of 3rd & 4th Raiding Regts
17× Type 100 transports
Bayug (Burauen North) airfield
72 men, 3rd Raiding Regt
6× Type 100 transports
San Pablo airstrip
24–36 men, 4th Raiding Regt
3× Type 100 transports
Dulag airfield
84 men, 4th Raiding Regt
20 men, 3rd Raiding Regt
7× Type 100 transports
2× Type 100 heavy bombers
Tacloban airfield
44 men, 4th Raiding Regt
2× Type 100 transports
2× Type 100 heavy bombers

LtGen Kyoji Tominaga, commanding 4th Air Army, shakes hands with the Kaoru Detachment's commander Lt Shigeo Naka as the raiders prepare to leave Lipa airfield, Luzon, for the *Gi* Operation to Leyte. The lieutenant has goggles fastened around his slung helmet.

The second echelon comprised the 3rd & Heavy Weapon Cos of 3rd Raiding Regt, and the signal unit; a third echelon consisted of the remaining 80 men.

Initially X-Day for the *Wa* Operation was set for December 5, in spite of the unreadiness of 16th and 26th Divisions. These commenced their attacks on the night of the 5th – never having been informed of a change of plan that would delay the airborne phase until the next night due to bad weather. On December 5 the transports arrived at Clark Field from Formosa, and were immediately camouflaged to avoid US air raids.

At 1540hrs on December 6, 35 transports and four heavy bombers took off from Clark Field. As soon as the formation was over Leyte AA fire began bursting around them. The transports bound for Burauen reached their area, but because enemy fire confused the pilots most paratroopers were dropped over San Pablo airstrip, with only Maj Shirai and about 60 men jumping on Buri. The transports bound for Dulag and Tacloban were all shot down.

Only 17 of the 35 transports returned to Lipa airfield, most of them damaged. The next day the second echelon's eight transports and two bombers took off, but bad weather over Leyte caused them to abort. Because of the US advance on Ormoc by the 1st Cavalry and 77th Inf Divs, further flights to Burauen were canceled.

Defending the Burauen area was the US 11th Airborne Div (MajGen Joseph M.Swing), which had landed by sea on November 18 to reinforce XXIV Corps. The division's elements were widely scattered in the rugged hills, and relied on the 35 single-engine L-4 liaison aircraft at Bayug to airdrop supplies. Elements of the 127th Engineer Bn and 408th Quartermaster and 511th Signal Cos were located beside Bayug, and the Division HQ and Division Artillery HQ were near San Pablo. The 1st Bn, 187th Glider Infantry was at Buri, and AA units to the west.

The Japanese transports appeared at 1800hrs on December 6, and parachutes blossomed over the airfields. Some 300 Japanese troops from the 16th Div also fought their way down from the hills and dug-in in a wooded area on the north side of Buri. Some paratroopers were shot down as they landed, but many managed to reach the packed lines of liaison aircraft at Bayug and began grenading them. Fuel and supply dumps were set on fire, and the raiders seized and used abandoned US weapons. They called out to the Americans to surrender, since it was futile to resist; but some 60 US supply men and ground crews dug-in on the south side of the Bayug strip and held out all night. Divisional HQ troops secured the San Pablo strip, while the 127th Engineers counter-attacked, fighting as infantry.

At daylight on December 7 the 674th Glider Field Artillery Bn, reorganized as infantry, arrived from the beach and joined the 127th in action. By nightfall on the 7th the engineers and gunners had secured much of the area and were dug-in north of the airfields. Flyable liaison aircraft took off to resume dropping supplies to frontline units. The 1st Bn, 187th Glider, with the aid of 1st Bn, 149th Infantry from 38th Inf Div and the 767th Tank Bn, continued mopping up until December 11. No raiders were taken prisoner.

The Japanese had counted on the shock effect of raiders parachuting from the sky, but this was lost on the 11th Airborne, to whom it appeared perfectly natural. Bottles of liquor were found on some of the Japanese dead, with instructions that it was not to be drunk until airborne. The raiders hoisted a Rising Sun flag on a palm tree beside the San Pablo strip, which two US soldiers cut down under fire. It was inscribed: "To Tsuneharu Shirai, Katori Shimpei. Exert your utmost for your country. Kyoji Tominaga, Lieutenant-General, December 3, 1944."[3]

After losing about half his men Maj Shirai withdrew from Buri and on December 8 went to Bayug, but found no comrades there. They returned to Buri, but after the second echelon failed to arrive they marched west overland, linking up with a unit from 26th Div on December 18.

Because many elements of different American units were committed piecemeal, it is unclear how many US casualties were caused. The loss of 11 liaison aircraft and some degree of damage to most others hampered the resupply of frontline units until they were replaced some days later.

The battle of Ormoc

Knowing the Americans had landed near Ormoc on December 7, the 4th Air Army dispatched the rest of the 4th Raiding Regt there. Between December 8 and 14, 481 paratroopers dropped on to Valencia airfield, 9 miles north of Ormoc. There were some 1,700 Japanese at Ormoc, mostly rear service troops, with only 350 men of the 12th Independent Inf Regt (the Imabori Unit).

The first 90 paratroopers of the 1st Co, 4th Raiding Regt jumped on Valencia on December 8 and rapidly moved south. They successfully attacked a US-held hill position east of Ormoc, but shellfire soon killed

---

3 This flag is now in the West Point Military Academy Museum. *Katori* was the codename of Maj Tsuneharu Shirai's 3rd Raiding Regt, and *Shimpei* was derived from the propaganda song *Sora no Shimpei*, "Soldier Gods of the Sky".

November 26, 1944: Lt Kaku supervises Kaoru raiders loading on to a Type 0 "Tabby" heavily camouflaged on the edge of Lipa airfield near Manila. Note the small rolled shelter cape carried on their backs, and the fact that most – e.g. left foreground – carry pouches for LMG magazines in addition to their Type 99 rifles.

the company commander, Lt Takakuwa, and half his men became casualties. After dark they withdrew and joined the Imabori Unit.

Bad weather on the 9th prevented flying; on the 10th, the regimental commander Maj Saida jumped in with 84 paratroopers of his 3rd Company. The 35th Army HQ attached his force to the Imabori Unit, and they took up position on a hillside above the road north of Ormoc. The next morning a US battalion attacked under cover of a heavy bombardment. At a critical moment Saida ordered a counter-attack; the 3rd Co commander, Lt Akashi, and his 70 men crept along a rice paddy ditch, emerging to charge the enemy at close range and forcing them to withdraw. Akashi's company were surrounded by a renewed American advance, however, and came under shellfire; Akashi vanished in an explosion (only his sword was found), and the company lost about one-third its strength. From this point the battered paratroopers conducted no further direct attacks; they remained dug-in by daylight, though after dark they conducted raids (kirikoni) to destroy ammunition and fuel dumps and steal food. The Japanese defense was broken on December 16 and US troops advanced towards Valencia. On December 20 the 35th Army ordered the remnants to retreat to the Canquipot Mountains; only about 100 of Maj Saida's surviving paratroopers reached there.

On the night of December 14, Capt Ohmura and 35 men of his Heavy Weapons Co, 4th Raiding Regt, had dropped near Valencia – the sixth and final party to jump, due to the impossibility of providing any more aircraft. They had a lucky escape when they jumped early, since Valencia was under bombardment. At 35th Army HQ they were sent north to Limon to link up with the exhausted Japanese 1st Div (LtGen Tadasu Kataoka.) Collecting survivors of his regiment's 3rd Co, Ohmura led 75 men north; Gen Kataoka was delighted to see these elite soldiers with their clean paratrooper uniforms and sub-machine guns. After

IJA paratroopers descend from "Topsy" transports using the Type 4 (1944) parachute, a parabolic design with cambered skirts to reduce oscillation – the swinging to which the earlier rigs were prone, and which could be fatal if a jumper struck the ground during a down-swing.

In recent years a myth has emerged that late in the war Japan was experimenting with "*kamikaze* skydivers*," who would strap on a bomb and freefall towards an Allied ship. A 50kg (110lb) bomb would have greatly hampered freefall maneuvering, and would have inflicted little damage – to say nothing of the fact that freefall parachuting was not developed until the late 1950s.

"Takachiho paratroopers" of the 2nd Raiding Bde study a terrain board representing the Burauen airfields on Leyte; the man at left holds an aerial photograph. They wear shirtsleeve tropical service uniform with standard rank patches on the collar, and the *hachimaki* headbands traditionally worn by warriors going into battle, to keep sweat out of their eyes and as a sign of determination. While certainly worn by *kamikaze* pilots, the *hachimaki* was not exclusive to them, as has been suggested.

delaying actions under heavy fire from US artillery, on the night of December 21 they were ordered to retreat, escorting the 1st Div HQ; they suffered repeated attacks by Filipino guerrillas armed with mortars, and only 47 of these paratroopers reached Canquipot on December 31. In January 1945, Ohmura's party was strengthened to 100-plus by paratroop stragglers and Kaoru unit survivors. Late in the month Maj Shirai brought in a dozen survivors of 3rd Raiding Regt; he himself was suffering from jaundice, and died a few days later. According to Capt Ohmura's account, the last survivors from 4th Raiding Regt brought total strength to about 400 paratroopers. Under repeated attack during February, the surrounded Japanese were steadily weakened by combat casualties, disease and hunger.

On March 17, Maj Saida, Capt Ohmura and 76 fit paratroopers were ordered to escort 35th Army HQ to the coast for shipping to Cebu. They had to abandon their wounded and sick, and lost more men during their evasion and march to the rendezvous. Only two of the expected four *Daihatsu* landing barges arrived, so half the party had to be left behind (none of the 100 paratroopers left on Leyte survived the war.) The two barges reached Tabogon on the north of Cebu, but were then destroyed by US PT boats; on March 24 the survivors rejoined 1st Div personnel at Cebu city. When the Americans landed on Cebu 35th Army HQ again escaped, using native canoes and escorted by Maj Saida and 20 paratroopers. On June 14 they were strafed at sea by a US fighter and Gen Suzuki and his staff were killed; Saida and a few paratroopers managed to reach Mindanao. Paratroopers remaining on Cebu joined 1st Div survivors who had also withdrawn from Leyte. They hid in the jungle to avoid US troops and Filipino guerrillas, but only 17 paratroopers on Cebu survived the war.

The 2nd Raiding Brigade after Leyte

After the main body of the 2nd Raiding Bde was sent to Leyte, about 500 of the Takachiho paratroopers remained on Luzon. Following the fall of Leyte, Allied landings on nearby islands were expected, and 4th Air Army dispatched a paratrooper detachment to Bacolod airfield on the north of Negros island. The Heavy Weapons Co, 3rd Raiding Regt formed the core, under Capt Honmura. While flying in on December 17 and 18, two transports were shot down by US fighters; about 60 paratroopers reached Bacolod. The Japanese 77th Inf Bde (–), detached from the 102nd Div on Cebu, was stationed on Negros; this was a second-line unit whose only combat experience had been against guerrillas. Their commander, MajGen Takeshi Kohno, welcomed the arrival of these elite soldiers and asked them to instruct his men in antitank tactics, and the demonstrations by the well-trained paratroopers made a great impression.

The US forces initially by-passed Negros and landed on Luzon. For over three months the paratroopers took part only in local anti-guerrilla operations, until March 29, 1945, when the US 40th Inf Div landed on the west coast and advanced towards Bacolod. The Japanese units deployed on the plain were pushed into the mountains, which offered excellent positions. On April 9 the Americans, reinforced by 503rd Parachute Inf Regt, launched an offensive. The Takachiho detachment opened fire on their counterpart paratroopers at close range; their defense against infantry and tanks was so determined that the Americans were unable to overrun their positions until June 2. Captain Honmura was killed; the surviving Japanese troops withdrew deeper into the mountains, and were only harassed by US patrols until the war's end. During that time thousands of the Negros garrison died of disease and starvation, and only 30 Takachiho paratroopers survived.

After the US landing on Luzon on January 9, 1945, the remaining men of 2nd Raiding Bde moved to Echague in the north, accompanying 4th Air Army HQ. In March they were ordered to Balete Pass and attached to the 10th Div (LtGen Yasuyuki Okamoto.) They resisted the US advance, but on May 27 the Americans broke through the pass and the Takachiho unit was left behind. They retreated eastwards into the Mamparang Mountains, where word reached them of Japan's surrender at the end of August, by which time only about 80 men survived.

THE 1st RAIDING GROUP ON LUZON

When the 1st Raiding Group was organized the 2nd Raiding Bde had already been sent to Luzon. Major-General Tsukada strongly requested IGHQ that his command be deployed to the Philippines; elements were subsequently sent to Luzon, but the 1st Raiding Bde, 1st Raiding Tank Unit, and 1st Raiding Maintenance Unit remained with the strategic reserve in Japan to form new parachute units.

The group's first echelon – 1st Glider Inf Regt and a company each from the 1st Raiding Engineer Unit and 1st Raiding Signal Unit – left Japan aboard the aircraft carrier *Unryu* on December 17. On the 19th, five torpedoes from the USS *Redfish* (SS-395) struck the carrier, and about 1,000 troops of the Raiding Group were lost. The second echelon – the 750-man 2nd Glider Inf Regt, 1st Raiding Engineer Unit (–), 1st Raiding Signal Unit (–), and 1st Raiding Machine Cannon Unit – departed Japan on December 21 and arrived safely at San Fernando, Luzon, on the 29th. The glider infantry moved south by rail to Clark Field. The other units were left at San Fernando when the railroad was cut by air raids; they joined the Shobu Group, and fought at Baguio.

General Tsukada and his staff flew into Clark Field on January 8, 1945, to find it in chaos. About 30,000 troops from different IJA, IJN, and air units swarmed all over the airbase with no one in overall command. General Tsukada was assigned to command the Kempu Group, with the 2nd Glider Inf Regt, 2nd Mobile Inf Regt, 39th Inf Regt (–), large numbers of 4th Air Army service troops, plus IJN antiaircraft, construction and air service personnel. Responsible for defending the Caraballo Mountains, including Clark Field, Gen Tsukada reorganized the units, developed a defense plan, and established defensive lines to the north, with the 2nd Glider Inf Regt in the center of the second line. He was all too aware of the difficulty of defending the vast complex of 11 airfields on an open plain.

The American XIV Corps attack began on January 23. General Tsukada held the first line until the 30th, when the survivors, overwhelmed by American firepower, pulled back to the second line. The US 40th Inf Div fought their way into the hills in savage combat; the Japanese glider troops resisted desperately, but their food and water ran out. On about February 10 they retreated to the wilderness of Mount Pinatubo and the Americans secured Clark Field. In recognition of his efforts Tsukada was promoted to lieutenant-general in March. His Kempu Group was attacked first by the US 43rd and later by the 38th Inf Div, and by early April it was greatly weakened. On April 6, Gen Tsukada ordered his units to disperse and

The commander of the 3rd Raiding Regt, Maj Tsuneharu Shirai (center), and his adjutant Capt Kohno, donning their equipment at Clark Field, Luzon, for the Burauen airfields operation of December 6, 1944. They will next put on their jump smocks, over their personal equipment.

fend for themselves. He himself surrendered on September 2 with some 1,500 men, of whom about 100 were from the 2nd Glider Inf Regiment.

THE GIRETSU AIRBORNE UNIT ON OKINAWA

On November 24, 1944, a formation of B-29 bombers inflicted the first raid on Tokyo from the Marianas; and the 1st Raiding Bde was ordered to form a special unit for a commando mission. Japanese bombing of the Marianas airfields was insufficient to delay the construction of USAAF bomber bases; the IGHQ planned to send airborne commandos to crash-land on the Saipan airfields and destroy the B-29s.

Captain Michiro Okuyama was selected to lead the special unit; he was the commander of the 1st Raiding Regt's Engineer Co, trained in sabotage and demolition techniques. Other soldiers of the regiment who had missed earlier operations were also eager for action. Captain Okuyama had been the first member of the original IJA parachute training unit; this outstanding and highly respected officer was entrusted by brigade HQ with choosing the 126 men for what he knew was a suicide mission. He selected most of them from his own company; later, the special team was named Giretsu Airborne Unit (*Giretsu Kuteitai*) – Giretsu means "respect for faith." It was organized as a command section (Capt Okuyama) and five platoons – 1st Plt (Lt Utsuki), 2nd (Lt Sugata), 3rd (Capt Watabe), 4th (Lt Murakami) and 5th (Lieutenant Yamada.)

Men of 2nd Raiding Bde go through the final steps of rigging their equipment. The central paratrooper is rolling up the lowering ropes for his leg bags – see Plate H2.

December 6, Clark Field: two fully loaded paratroopers await the order to board the aircraft for Leyte. The medical aid man (*eiseihei*) has haversacks packed with medical supplies rigged as leg bags; note that the Japanese, like Christian nations, used the red cross emblem.

On December 5 the unit moved to the IJA air academy at Saitama, Kanto. There ten intelligence officers, experts in sabotage, joined them from the Nakano intelligence school; two were assigned to each platoon, bringing total strength to 136. The unit was placed under the direct command of the Leading Air Army. At Saitama a mock-up of a B-29 was prepared. Type 99 magnetic charges could not clamp to the aircraft's aluminum skin, so two types of special weapons were developed. One had a 2kg (4.4lb) explosive charge at the end of a pole; a rubber suction cup was attached on the top of the charge. Gripping the pole, the raider pushed it up under the B-29's wing, and pulled a cord to ignite the delay fuse. The other weapon was the chain charge, a 13–16ft rope with explosive charges attached along its length; a small sandbag weight was attached to one end, to aid throwing it over the aircraft's fuselage or wing.

The Giretsu commandos began intense training; Capt Okuyama stressed that each man must destroy two or three planes at least, even if he was mortally wounded in the process. On December 22 the Giretsu Unit conducted a demonstration for senior staff; the commandos ran swiftly through the darkness as though it were daylight, and skilfully attached their explosives to planes. The observers were impressed by a performance worthy of *Ninjas*.

Although the Giretsu commandos were ready, the preparation of the air transport unit was delayed. The 3rd Independent Flying Unit (Capt Suwabe) was assigned to deliver the Giretsu Unit, converting from their previous Type 100 scout aircraft on to Mitsubishi Type 97 "Sally"

bombers. The pilots were inexperienced with these new aircraft and not yet able to conduct long range flights over water. The attack was nevertheless scheduled for January 17, 1945, and the commandos moved to Hamamatsu airbase on Honshu. However, American raids damaged the planned refueling airfields on Iwo Jima (Type 97 bombers had insufficient range to fly to the Marianas direct from Japan), and the operation was canceled. The disappointed Giretsu commandos returned to Nyutabaru and the 1st Raiding Brigade.

After the Marianas raid was canceled plans were made to attack airfields on Iwo Jima captured by the US Marines in March, but these too were canceled when the Iwo Jima garrison fell. The Giretsu Airborne Unit was not disbanded, however, and the commandos remained willing and ready. This period was difficult for them: as a suicide unit they were especially well treated, but these privileges were a burden for the waiting commandos. On April 1, US forces landed on Okinawa, and American fighters deployed to the captured Yontan (Japanese, Yomitan) and Kadena airfields on Okinawa's west coast intercepted and shot down many *kamikaze* planes attacking the American fleet. On May 15, 6th Air Army (former Leading Air Army) requested that IGHQ allow the use of the Giretsu Unit to neutralize these airfields.

The commandos and the 3rd Independent Flying Unit moved to Kengun airfield on Kyushu to prepare for what was designated the *Gi* Operation. The flying unit provided 16x Type 97 bombers and four in reserve, stripped of guns to save weight. Eight would carry Capt Okuyama with his 1st, 2nd & 5th Plts to Yontan; another four were assigned to take Capt Watabe and 3rd & 4th Plts to Kadena. The plan was for the force to take off from Kengun in the evening, and crash-land on the US airfields before midnight. The raiders would destroy aircraft and facilities, then take up positions nearby to prevent enemy use of the airfields with automatic weapons fire. Almost 50 IJA and IJN bombers and fighters would attack the target airfields before the commandos landed, in hope of distracting the Americans from the approach of the raiders' aircraft. Next day, with the US fighter fields neutralized, some 180 IJN and IJA *kamikazes* and over 30 conventional attack aircraft (some bearing *Ohka* piloted flying bombs) would attack US shipping.

The detailed organization of the Giretsu Unit was as follows; besides the listed weapons, each commando carried HE and WP grenades plus a pistol:

Command Section (10 men)
　　LMG team (1× LMG)
　　Messenger team
　　Signal team
1st–5th Platoons, each of two *Sections*, each of:
　　1st Team (4 men including section leader): 1× Type 99 rifle, 2× Type 100 SMGs, 2× pole charges, 4× Type 99 AT charges
　　2nd Team (3 men): 1× rifle, 1× Type 99 LMG, 1× pole charge, 4× Type 99 AT charges
　　3rd Team (3 men): 1× rifle, 1× SMG, 1× pole charge, 4× Type 99 AT charges
　　4th Team (3 men): 1× rifle, 1× SMG, 1× Type 89 grenade discharger, 1× pole charge, 4× Type 99 AT charges

The attack was planned for May 23, but bad weather over Okinawa forced its postponement by a day. When the commandos assembled on the airfield their spirits were high, although they did not expect to return. After a brief ceremony they boarded the planes, and at 1850hrs on May 24 the 12 bombers took off and headed southwest on the 480-mile flight to Okinawa; four of them aborted, however, returning to base with engine problems.

On the departure airbase men waited around a speaker connected to the radio room. At 2210hrs they heard a message from the Giretsu Unit – "Now, I land!' – and they shouted with joy. About a half-hour later US radio traffic indicated an emergency at Yontan airfield, where Japanese aircraft reported a huge fire.

As *kamikazes* attacked radar picket ships, attack aircraft made their runs on the airfields beginning at 2000hrs, and in their wake the bombers

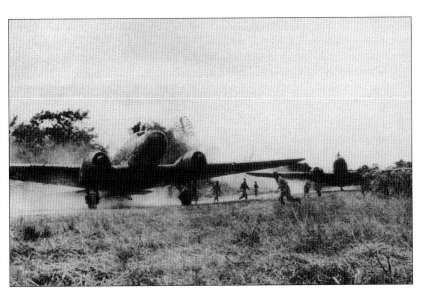

1540 hrs, December 6: 35 Type 100 "Topsy" transports and four Type 100 "Helen" bombers run up for take-off from Clark Field, to fly 270 miles southeast to Negros. There they would rendezvous with fighter escorts and light bombers from Bacolod airfield, and turn east for the last 140 miles to Leyte and the US-held Burauen airfield complex, through clear skies.

carrying the Giretsu commandos roared in at low level. US Marine and Army AA battalions opened fire, downing 11 twin-engine aircraft. Bombs intended for Yontan, the base for Marine Air Group 31, missed the airfield. At 2125 a "Sally" made a run much lower than previous attacks, and was shot down. At 2230 three more approached, apparently trying to land; they too were brought down, crashing near the field, but a small number of the Japanese commandos survived and rushed to accomplish their mission. One bomber's wing struck an AA gun position, burying the crew and killing two of them. A fifth "Sally" belly-landed on the NW/SE runway, sliding to a halt 80 yards from the control tower; an estimated 12 commandos dashed from this plane, throwing grenades and demolition charges and firing their weapons. Two fuel dumps were set alight, with the loss of 70,000 gallons. Pandemonium reigned as Marine ground crewmen, AA gunners and security troops opened fire in all directions; this indiscriminate firing caused most of the Americans' 18 wounded and one killed, and some of the aircraft damage.

All of the commandos were killed, the last being discovered at 1255hrs the next day hiding in the brush. In all, 69 Japanese commandos and airmen were buried; some had committed suicide. US aircraft losses were three F4U Corsair fighters, two four-engine PB4Y Privateer patrol bombers, and four R4D (C-47) transports. Another 22 F4Us, three F6F Hellcat fighters, two PB4Ys and two R4Ds were damaged.

Japanese *kamikaze* attacks were launched on May 25 and 27, but it could not be determined by the Japanese if the Yontan attack had had a significant effect on the numbers of American fighters defending the fleet, large numbers of which were still available. Yontan was operational again on the afternoon of the 25th, and most damaged aircraft were repaired within days.

The last of Japan's paratroopers

Some months later another airborne raid on the Okinawa airfields was planned. This time it was intended to airlift 12 Type 95 light trucks armed with 2cm Type 98 machine cannons, by bomber-towed Ku-8 gliders. The drivers were selected from the 1st Raiding Tank Unit and

The IJN used their long-ranged Mitsubishi G4M Type 1 "Betty" heavy bomber to drop cargo containers for paratroopers and to transport raiders. This example has an Ohka piloted rocket-propelled bomb fitted to the belly. A suicide mission by 60 G4Ms carrying 300 paratroopers of 1st Raiding Regt to the Marianas airfields was planned for August 19, 1945, but was aborted by the Japanese surrender.

gunners from other 1st Raiding Bde units, and Capt Toshio Hirota of the tank unit was chosen to command. Early in August 1945 they moved to Fussa airfield near Tokyo; the attack was to be carried out at the end of August, but on the 15th of that month Japan announced its intention to surrender.

The IJN planned an attack similar to the Giretsu Unit's aborted raid on the Marianas B-29 airfields, designated the *Ken* Operation. Some 300 sailors of LtCdr Daiji Yamaoka's Kure 101st SNLF began preparations at the end of June; this unit was formed as a "submarine SNLF" intended to land on enemy-held islands, but on this occasion they would be carried aboard 30 Type 1 "Betty" bombers, whose long range (3,750 miles) allowed a one-way mission to the Marianas. The raid was initially planned for July 24, but on July 14 American carrier planes raided Misawa naval airbase, Honshu, where the operation's bombers were destroyed or damaged. The raid was postponed until August 19. Although the plan was conceived by the IJN, at the end of July the IGHQ ordered that 300 1st Raiding Regt paratroopers under Capt Sunao Sonoda be included and 60 bombers readied. Again, Japan's surrender canceled the operation.

This Type 97 "Sally" heavy bomber of the 3rd Independent Flying Unit skidded to a halt near the Yontan airfield control tower on Okinawa on the night of May 24, 1945. It was the 12 Giretsu commandos who rode in this aircraft that caused most of the damage that night.

SELECT BIBLIOGRAPHY

Akimoto, Minoru, *Rakkasan Butai ('Paratroopers')* (Tokyo, R.Shuppan, 1972)

Daugherty, Leo J. III, *Fighting Techniques of a Japanese Infantryman, 1941–1945: Training, Techniques, and Weapons* (St Paul, MN: MBI Publishing, 2002)

Forty, George, *Japanese Army Handbook, 1939–1945* (Stroud, UK: Sutton Publishing, 1999)

Kaigun Rakkasankai, *Rakkasan Kisyu Butai ('Parachute Raiding Forces')* (Tokyo: Sobunsha, 1990)

Long, Gavin M., *The Six Years War: A Concise History of Australia in the 1939–1945 War* (Canberra: Australian War Memorial & Australian Government Publishing Service, 1973)

Nakanishi, Ritta, *Japanese Military Uniforms, 1930–1945* (Tokyo: Dai Nihon Kaiga, 1991)

Nakata, Tadao, *Imperial Japanese Army and Navy Uniforms and Equipment* (London: Arms & Armour Press, 1975; published in Japan as *Dainippon Teikoku Rikukaigun "Gunso to Sobi"*, Nakata Shoten, 1973)

O'Brien, Jerry T., *Giretsu: Japanese Commando Raid on Marine Positions during World War II* (Surprise, AZ: Equidata Publishing Company, 2006)

Rottman, Gordon L., *World War II Pacific Island Guide: a Geo-Military Study* (Westport, CT: Greenwood Publishing, 2002)

Tanaka, Kenichi, *Ohzora no Hana, Kutei Butai Zenshi ('Flower of the Sky, the History of Airborne Forces')* (Tokyo: Fuyo Shobo, 1984)

US Military Intelligence Division, *Japanese Parachute Troops*, Special Series No.32, 1 July 1944 (r/p Wickenburg, AZ: Normount Technical Publications, 1973)

US War Department, *Handbook on Japanese Military Forces*, TM-E 30-480, 15 September 1944, with Change 3, 1 June 1945, & Change 6, 15 September 1945 (r/p, without changes, London, Greenhill Books, 1991)

Yamabe, Masao, *Kaigun Rakkasan Butai ('Navy Paratroopers')* (Tokyo: Konnichi no Wadaisha, 1985)

THE PLATES

A: IMPERIAL JAPANESE ARMY PARATROOPS

A1: Paratrooper in training, 1941

He wears the lightweight one-piece jump suit with integral cloth belt, a large slanted zip-fastened pocket on the left chest only, and elasticated cuffs and ankles; rank patches were sometimes displayed on the collar. The helmet, of cloth-covered rubber, bears the universal IJA insignia of a yellow five-point star. The ankle boots are slightly higher versions of the standard issue, with seven rather than five pairs of eyelets; unlined leather summer-issue aircrew gloves were also worn. He wears the Type 1 (1941) parachute, without a chest reserve pack.

A2: Paratrooper, 2nd Raiding Regiment; Palembang operation, February 1942

The cloth-covered steel jump helmet was worn on operations. The IJA tested a sleeveless jump smock, with long zipped vents up the sides, but for operations they adopted this long-sleeved version without vents. Clearly modeled on that of the German *Fallschirmjäger*, it was worn over the personal equipment and standard field uniforms, complete with long puttees. For this attack the reserve pack was worn on the chest harness; for other operations it was discarded, since the low-altitude jumps would not have allowed time for its deployment, and weapon or equipment packs were attached instead.

A3: Paratroop officer on operations, 1942

This illustrates the back of the Type 1 parachute pack as worn. Some officers displayed a white disc on the back of the helmet for quick identification in combat.

A4, A5: Insignia were rarely worn on the smock, and only occasionally even when on home service. The IJA parachute qualification "wings" badge, instituted in September 1941, was the Golden Kite (*Kinshi Kunsho*), the messenger of the gods which legend says hovered over the battlefield dazzling the Emperor Jimmu Tenno's enemies with its golden wings. It was worn centered on the upper right sleeve. The red insignia of the 1st Raiding Brigade (later, Group) might be worn on the left sleeve.

B: 2ND RAIDING REGIMENT AT PALEMBANG, SUMATRA; FEBRUARY 14, 1942

Paratroopers of 1st Company fight their way off the DZ near Aerodrome P1; this group are more fortunate than others in that they have recovered a weapons container. **B1** has discarded his harness, reserve pack and smock, revealing his Type 98 (1938) summer cotton field uniform and personal equipment; he is still armed only with his Nambu Taisho Type 14 pistol. **B2**, who has put his belt equipment over his smock, is pulling Type 97 HE hand grenades from a haversack. **B3** is opening a 50kg Type 3 cargo container – see also Plate E7 – holding rifles, cushioned with cotton bags.

C: PARATROOPERS' WEAPONS

All paratroopers jumped with an 8mm semi-automatic pistol, either the Type 94 (1934) (**C1**), or Type 14 (1925) (**C2**); a Meiji Type 30 (1897) bayonet with 15¹⁄₈in blade (**C3**); and at least two HE grenades, Type 97 (1937) (**C4**) or Type 99 (1939) (**C5**). The 2lb 11oz Type 99 (1939) magnetic antiarmor charge (**C6**), used for attacking tanks and the steel doors and shutters of pillboxes, was issued in a pouch, with the fuse/detonator packed inside in a two-piece metal tube; the fuse was screwed into the *99 hako-bakurai*, and the igniter struck against a solid object to initiate a 10-second delay.

The IJN initially used the 6.5mm Meiji Type 38 (1905) carbine (**C7**). Modified "take-down" (*tera*) rifles for paratroopers first appeared in 1942/43. A 1941 prototype of the Type 38 carbine with a hinged butt proved too fragile to be adopted. The first IJA attempt to develop a rifle that could be carried on the jump was the 7.7mm Type 100 (1940) – the Type 99 short rifle modified with a detachable barrel; the locking mechanism was inadequate, and only small numbers were issued. An improved purpose-made version was adopted as the Type 2 (1942) (**C8**, **C9** & **C10**) in May 1943, and was widely issued to IJA and IJN parachute units from late 1943. Take-down rifles were carried on the jump either in a canvas chest bag, or separated in two leg bags lowered on a short rope after the

An IJA 50kg (110lb) cargo parachute, made in June 1944 by Kokka Koku Heiki. The dark tan pack measures 17in × 9in × 6in; the white static line is stowed under the pin release flap, and the rope loops at the corners are for attaching to the cargo container. Just visible above the label is the black IJA stamp of a five-point open star in a circle. (Velmer Smith Collection)

parachute opened. The Type 1 (1941) paratrooper bandoleer (**C11**), of canvas and leather, was worn around the lower torso; it had seven pockets each holding two five-round rifle charger clips, and two grenade pockets – grenades were carried upside down, so leather bottom extensions accommodated the fuses.

D: IMPERIAL JAPANESE NAVY PARATROOPERS
D1: Paratrooper, barracks dress, 1942
Navy paratroopers wore this light cap, resembling a field cap but with a side-and-neck piece – note earholes – and chin strap, under their steel helmet; note the IJN yellow anchor badge. Their special clothing served as both a jump suit and combat uniform. This version of the jacket had an angled pistol pocket on the right chest and a two-grenade pocket on the left; the other had two large bellows pockets on the chest, and three small pockets on each side of the skirt for ammunition or grenades. The snap-secured chest pockets were placed low to accommodate the positioning of the parachute harness. Variations were also seen in the number and layout of the ample pockets provided on the trousers for a first aid kit, compressed rations, semaphore flags (red and white) and other

An IJN 50kg cargo parachute. The circular pack is dark green with orange edge binding; the rope loops for attachment are white, and in this case the static line has been cut off close to the pin protector flap. (Yokohama WWII Japanese Military Radio Museum)

small items. The trousers, supported by waist tie-tapes and suspenders, were close-fitting to prevent snagging, and had rubber instep straps to retain them inside high-top jump boots. His undershirt is standard IJN issue. Enlisted men's rating patches were displayed on the right sleeve.

D2: Paratrooper on operations, 1942
The same uniform is worn, with the steel helmet tied in place with tapes over the cap. The Type 1 harness is used, with the Navy Type 1 Special pack – see Plate E4. On the ground is a rigid parachute carrying case; for the IJN these were dark green or olive drab, for the IJA initially orange but from 1942 light tan or olive drab.

D3: Paratrooper on operations, 1942 (rear)
This illustrates the Navy Type 1 Special parachute pack. As on A3, note the quilted backpad.

D4: Paratrooper's rating patches
The IJN's circular patches – in red-on-blue or, for summer, black-on-white – were replaced in November 1942 with squared shield-shape patches. No paratrooper's patches were produced in the new style, since the branch was at that date disbanding. 3rd, 2nd & 1st Class seamen rates wore a single branch symbol, crossed symbols, and crossed symbols below a blossom respectively; 3rd, 2nd & 1st Class petty officers wore the same but within a wreath.

E: PARACHUTES & CARGO CONTAINER
Most parachutes were produced by Fujikura Aircraft Industry Co Ltd. While wartime shortage forced Western nations to

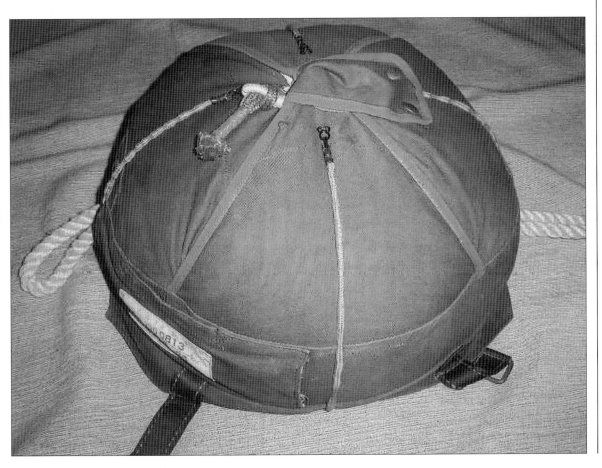

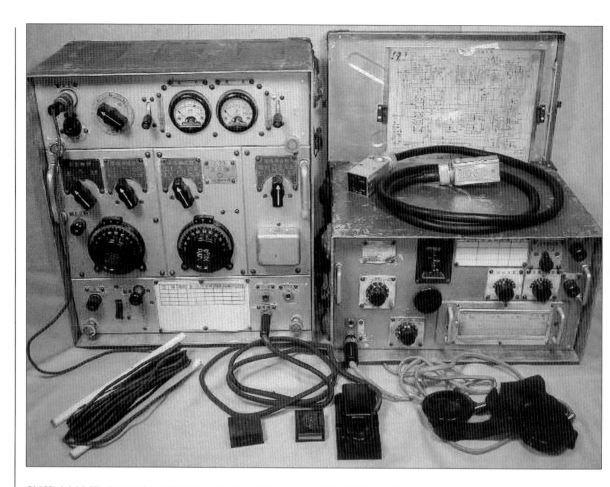

Chi **Model 95 Mk 4 ground-to-air radio as used by IJA paratroopers – transmitter unit on left, receiver on right. The inner surfaces are bright metal, the outer painted brownish olive drab; dial rims, knobs, switches and turrets are black; the four arch-shaped labels on the transmitter are black, red, green and red, from left to right. Accessories include a wire antenna on a spool, Morse code key, and earphone set. This equipment, with a range of around 60 miles, was not available for the Palembang operation in February 1942; on that occasion the *Tobi* Mk 1 radio as used in scout planes was modified for ground use. (Yokohama WWII Japanese Military Radio Museum)**

change from silk canopies to rayon or nylon, Japan continued to use white silk, and did not adopt subdued colors. The cotton canvas packs were required to be repacked monthly even if not used. Materials and workmanship remained of high standard; harness webbing was of a 3,000lb-test silk/cotton blend, and fittings were of chromium-plated steel.

E1: IJA Type 1 (1941) main parachute
Army packs were orange with dark green tape trim and reinforcement, orange bungees, and yellow static line.

E2: IJA Type 1 reserve pack
The chest pack was in the same colors, with a red ripcord.

E3: IJN Type 1 reserve pack
Navy parachute packs were in reversed colors from IJA rigs, and were stamped with a black anchor.

E4: IJN Type 1 Special main parachute
This differed in having a single suspension point centrally behind the shoulders.

E5: IJA Type 4 (1944) main parachute
E6: IJA Type 4 main parachute harness
Some late war IJA packs were also seen in dark tan or olive drab.

E7: IJA 50kg (110lb) cargo container
About 42in long, this aluminum case was of rectangular section with rounded corners, painted light olive drab with steel gray fittings and brown leather securing straps. The bottom end was fitted with a canvas-covered cushion; the parachute pack attached at the top with rope loops and toggles. The load – in this case, entrenching spades – was protected by white cushion bags.

F: YOKOSUKA 1ST SNLF AT MANADO, CELEBES; JANUARY 11, 1942
After landing on Langoan airfield the 1st Company had little difficulty finding their weapons containers. **F1** carries the IJN paratrooper's 6.5mm Meiji Type 38 (1905) carbine, to which he has fixed the Type 30 bayonet; he carries 85 rounds of ammunition in crossed 17-pocket bandoleers. **F2** is using the 5cm Type 89 grenade discharger, and carries its ammunition in two four-pocket pouch sets looped on to his belt and supported by canvas braces. **F3** is an empty IJN cylindrical 30kg (66lb) cargo container, in unpainted aluminum; this measured 42in by 14 inches. Note red identification bands, green web securing strap, and IJN cargo parachute pack.

G: PARATROOPERS' WEAPONS

The standard 7.7mm Type 99 (1939) LMG, which already had a detachable quick-change barrel, was provided with a detachable shoulder stock and hollow forward-folding pistol grip; this model came into use in 1943 (**G1, G2**). At 46¹/₂in long, this weighed 23lb, took 30-round box magazines, and had a rate of fire of 850rpm. Few sub-machine guns were initially used, but larger numbers were issued for the deployments to the Philippines in 1944; although they were not listed on organization tables, a Takachiho paratrooper veteran stated that they had about 100 per regiment. Three versions of the 8mm Type 100 (1940) were employed. The original 1940 version (**G3**), which already had a detachable barrel, was modified in 1942 with a folding stock and the removal of the flash hider (**G4a, 4b**); length was 34in, or 22.2in folded; weight, 7¹/₂lb; and rate of fire, 450rpm. The much altered 1944 version (**G5**), without a folding stock, weighed 8¹/₂lb, measured 36in, and fired at 850rpm. All used 30-round magazines. The Type 100 bayonet issued with the SMG had an 8in blade (**G6**). The 5cm Type 89 (1929) grenade discharger (**G7**) – popularly but mistakenly called a "knee mortar" by Allied troops – weighed 10.3lb; a 1943 paratroop version had a detachable base plate (**G8**), although the standard model base plate and firing mechanism could already be unscrewed and reversed inside the barrel for compact carrying. This valuable weapon fired HE (**G9a**) or WP (**G9b**) shells out to 700yds, and Type 91 (1931) hand grenades fitted with propellant charges (**G9c**) to 200yds; a range of smoke and pyrotechnic rounds included this 3-star red flare (**G9d**). The discharger was carried in a canvas case slung from the shoulder, and paratroopers were provided with a chest pack. Some IJA officers carried 3.5cm Taisho Type 10 (1921) flare pistols (**G10**); the IJN used the 2.8cm Type 97 (1937) (**G11**). The IJN 17-pocket paratroop bandoleer is shown at (**G12**).

H: IJA AIRBORNE TROOPS, 1944–45

H1: Takasago guerrilla, Kaoru Airborne Raiding Detachment; Clark Field, Luzon, November 26, 1944

Lightly equipped for his one-way mission, this raider wears a camouflage cover and net on his standard issue steel helmet, and standard field uniform, here with the rank patches of first class private. Enlisted ranks wore a white armband on the right arm for night identification, and NCOs and officers a white sash from shoulder to hip. They were armed with Type 99 short rifles and Type 99 LMGs; many carried extra LMG magazines in canvas and leather pouches slung on the hip. The Formosan tribesmen also carried their traditional *giyuto* sidearm. Demolition charges and grenades were carried in chest haversacks; pistols, ammunition and grenades in Type 1 bandoleers; rations and small kit items in a second haversack on the right hip, with a water canteen; and a rolled shelter cape was slung on the back.

H2: Paratrooper, 2nd Raiding Brigade; Clark Field, Luzon, December 6, 1944

For the December 6 raid on the Burauen airfields, elements

IJN paratroopers required a lightweight radio, but these were not available for the 1942 Dutch East Indies operations. Late that year this experimental set was developed; it did not see use in paratroop operations, but may have been employed by other SNLFs. It measures 8½ × 8 × 2¾in, and is painted dark green with white markings. (Yokohama WWII Japanese Military Radio Museum)

of 3rd & 4th Raiding Regts wore new equipment and, for the first time, jumped carrying their primary weapons. The cloth-covered helmet and the clothing were unchanged. Apart from Type 2 rifle, Type 99 LMG or Type 100 SMG ammunition, each man carried two hand grenades, two AT grenades, two smoke candles, two Type 99 magnetic charges, six demolition charges, a shovel and 100 feet of rope. Take-down weapons were divided between two leg bags, and additional haversacks were sewn to wide bands encircling the ankles. When the canopy opened the paratrooper pulled a quick-release knot in the tapes securing the leg bags, and lowered them on 3m ropes. This man is stowing three-clip cartons of rifle ammunition. His parachute is the new Type 4 (1944.)

H3: Volunteer, Giretsu Airborne Unit; Kengun airfield, Kyushu, May 24, 1945

The unit were photographed on the airfield before embarking. They wore field caps rather than helmets, and tropical field uniforms self-camouflaged with streaks of black and dark green paint. At least one man in each of the three-man teams that made up each section carried a pole charge. Each man carried a canteen, a haversack with rations, and a backpack for the Type 99 charges. The often pictured "Type 2 bandoleer" was in fact a leather service belt reversed and fitted with canvas pouches for Type 99 grenades, a canvas pistol holster and three-pocket pistol magazine pouch.

H4: Unidentified patch

This insignia was reported in 1944; it may be IJA, but its exact meaning and use are unconfirmed.

INDEX